Table of Contents

Introduction

Afghanistan has become the hub of global terrorism over the past twenty years and plays host to multiple *Salafi* factions that enjoy a sense of security and freedom of movement, mainly because of the permissive environment and porous borders between Afghanistan and Pakistan.[1] The Taliban in Afghanistan and Pakistan fight United States and NATO Coalition forces, but the group's interests are strictly local. The Taliban fights for survival and to achieve its goal of regaining control of the government. Unlike the Taliban with its local objective, *Al Qaeda* is a global terrorist organization that poses a direct and expressed threat to the United States and its interests around the world. But the real threat to America and the West is not a group or a person – it is an ideology based on the desire to bring the world to a state of authentic Islam.

American leadership has recently renewed its interest in the almost nine-year US conflict in Afghanistan, with the United States President appointing a new military commander in Afghanistan and approving a surge in ground forces aimed at defeating the insurgency and stabilizing the Afghan national government. With this increased focus, United States military and government leaders must have a better understanding of the environment, history, culture, and opposition – both internal and against Western involvement – in order to formulate the best possible operational and strategic goals and envision an acceptable outcome for US operations in Afghanistan.

A study of Islamic history in relation to the statements made by *Al Qaeda* reveal not only the group's strategy but a vision of its desired end state. This monograph argues that by understanding the ideological nature of the *Al Qaeda jihad*, United States political and military

---

[1]"Afghanistan's borders are open to the *mujahidin*. There are over three hundred kilometers of open borders, not to mention that surrounding the country are tribal regions that the authorities have not subjugated and that form a shield for the *mujahidin*." Abdallah Azzam, "The Defense of Muslim Territories Constitutes the First Individual Duty." In Gilles Kepel and Jean-Pierre Milelli, eds., *Al Qaeda in its Own Words* , trans. Pascale Ghazaleh (Cambridge, Mass.: Belknap Press of Harvard University Press, 2008), 108-109.

leaders will better formulate plans and develop operations that counter the effectiveness of *Al Qaeda's* words and actions. Osama bin Laden has made numerous statements about his aims and intentions and applied consistent effort toward achieving those ends. Knowing *Al Qaeda's* historical background and the core ideological beliefs and goals of its leadership facilitates a clearer understanding of how and why the group operates the way it does. Developing this understanding could provide insights into countering and defeating the *Al Qaeda* threat.

Today *Al Qaeda* has bases in several countries and conducts operations around the world, but this paper focuses on Afghanistan and Pakistan – the original base and current home of *Al Qaeda* leaders – and the threat the group's end state poses to the United States. Osama bin Laden established *Al Qaeda* during the 1979-1989 Soviet Afghan War, and the monograph briefly examines the different *jihadist* organizations that emerged from this war. This paper is not meant to serve as a detailed history of the region, but instead provides relevant historical context as it develops the conditions leading to the formation of *Al Qaeda*. The paper presents bin Laden's *jihadist* narrative as the continuation of a centuries-old Islamic struggle between perceived internal and external forces of corruption and achievement of a pure and authentic Muslim society, and about what actions make someone a true Muslim.

The research traces the sources of *Al Qaeda's* ideology from the Prophet Muhammad in the seventh century through bin Laden's mentor and partner Dr. Abdallah Azzam and examines how specific individuals contributed to the core beliefs espoused by *Al Qaeda* leaders bin Laden and Dr. Ayman al-Zawahiri. The purpose of this research is to show how core Islamic concepts and ideals of the past influence the current conflict in Afghanistan and Pakistan. The monograph then uses the results of the research as the basis for operational and strategic recommendations for United States leadership to pursue in Afghanistan to more effectively counter the *jihadist* ideology. First the paper explains a number of key terms that both Muslims and Westerners use to describe or define certain Islamic actors.

Extremist or Purist? Do These Labels Aid in Understanding?

> If preparing [for *jihad*] is terrorism, then we are terrorists. If defending our honor is extremism, then we are extremists. If *jihad* against our enemies is fundamentalism, then we are fundamentalists.
> - Dr. Abdallah Azzam, *From Secularism to Jihad*

Western books and media sources are filled with labels – like radical, or extremist, or fundamentalist – that aim to describe and define the enemy. In reality these words more often confuse rather than inform. The US administration continues to deal with issues of word choice in strategy and other official documents. In 2005 President George W. Bush shifted from using the phrase "global war on terrorism" to a "struggle against violent extremism."[2] In April 2010 as US forces prepare to surge in Afghanistan, White House sources leaked President Barack Obama's plan to ban certain terms including Islamic extremism, Islamic *jihad*, and Islamic fundamentalism from the National Security Strategy.[3] The US administration is now looking for ways to "counter violent extremism." It would be useful here to better explain some of these terms before getting into a deeper discussion of *jihad*. It is important to keep in mind that Westerners and Muslims can derive different meanings from these words.

Fundamentalism denotes a search for authenticity.[4] The term emerged in the West in the early twentieth century as a reference to evangelical Protestant Christians, but has since taken on a derogatory meaning that is often associated with Islamists and terrorism.[5] Core *Al Qaeda* member Ayman al-Zawahiri used the term fundamentalist throughout his book *Knights Under the*

---

[2]Steve Inskeep, "Shifting Language: Trading Terrorism for Extremism," NPR.com, July 27, 2005, http://www.npr.org/templates/story/story.php?storyId=4772826 (accessed April 13, 2010).

[3]Associated Press, "Obama Bans Islam, *Jihad* from National Security Strategy Document," FoxNews.com, April 7, 2010, http://www.foxnews.com/politics/2010/04/07/obama-bans-islam-jihad-national-security-strategy-document/ (accessed April 12, 2010).

[4]"The search for an 'authentic' way of acting in the Islamic world means that other paths, such as just being a Muslim or embracing Western values, are deficient or insufficient." Robert D. Lee, *Overcoming Tradition and Modernity: The Search for Islamic Authenticity* (Boulder: Westview Press, 1997), 175.

Prophet's Banner, noting it was a term Western forces used to label their Islamic enemy.[6]

According to noted Middle East historian Bernard Lewis, "Muslim fundamentalists are those who feel that the troubles of the Muslim world at the present time are the result not of insufficient modernization but of excessive modernization, which they see as a betrayal of authentic Islamic values."[7] Fundamentalists believe the solution to society's problems lies in a return to true Islam and restoration of Islamic Holy Law – *shari'a*. Because Westerners associate a negative meaning with fundamentalism, the term is not useful for improving understanding about Islam. Many Muslims are fundamentalists, but not all Muslims are terrorists or *jihadists* – the difference lies in how a fundamentalist expresses his belief.[8] Fundamentalists range the spectrum of action from internal devotion, to promotion of the Islamic faith through charity and education, to more violent demonstrations like suicide attacks.

Westerners often apply the term extremist to someone who is willing to use violence in the name of Islam, someone on the far end of the spectrum. A Muslim has a different point of view than a Westerner about what is extreme and what is moderate. In some cases, for example Wahhabism, what the West views as extreme has become mainstream in parts of the Islamic world. Muslim responses to the question "What is Islamic extremism?" on the *Sunni Forum* blog site illuminate a different perspective. One blogger described Islamic extremism as "a new term

---

[5]"The associations of irrational commitment, fanaticism, militancy, and terrorism make fundamentalism a useful term. It allows a dominant Western culture and society, aggressively led by the United States, to demonize its opponents as irretrievably antagonistic to the hegemonic values of ''freedom'' and ''democracy.'' ...However, the use of ''fundamentalism'' is itself an imposition of a term that comes from within Western Christian culture. Thus, the way in which opposition is characterized within Christianity becomes a way of dealing with opposition in other situations, whether religious, political, or cultural conflict." Tony Bennett, Lawrence Grossberg, and Meaghan Morris, eds., *New Keywords: A Revised Vocabulary of Culture and Society* (Oxford: Blackwell Publishing Ltd, 2005), 19.

[6]Gilles Kepel and Jean-Pierre Milelli, eds. *Al Qaeda in its Own Words,* trans. Pascale Ghazaleh (Cambridge, Mass.: Belknap Press of Harvard University Press, 2008), 193.

[7]Bernard Lewis, *The Crisis of Islam: Holy War and Unholy Terror* (New York: Modern Library, 2003), 134.

[8]Ibid, 137.

created by the West to classify some people into the same category as terrorists... giving them ample justification to oppress [Muslims]."[9] Another response was that the West invented the term extremist in order to "...create desired space to ascertain the accuracy of their...weapons."[10] One respondent posted that for Muslims the term extremist could apply to a non-practicing Muslim or one who does not strictly adhere to all aspects of the faith, to which another blogger replied that the West would call those Muslims "moderates" or "reformers."[11] The American view of moderate equates to a Muslim view of extremist, and often the opposite is true as well. Because the term extremist conveys significantly different meanings for Westerners and Muslims, using this term automatically creates tension and divisiveness between the two.

Islamism is inherently a political ideology and is closely related to fundamentalism. Islamist movements, like the Muslim Brotherhood, developed in the twentieth century in response to modernity and Westernization, especially against the idea of separating religion from public life. Islam is more than a religion, it is a way of life. Islam encompasses and guides all aspects of society – from legal and economic decisions, to education, and even to warfare. According to Ray Takeyh and Nikolas Gvosdev, authors of *The Receding Shadow of the Prophet*, "Islamists are those who believe that their particular vision of Islam must be implemented as a corrective to un-Islamic practices that have crept into the governments and economies... of the Muslim world."[12] There are three major forms of Islamism: moral Islamism, in which the Islamists try to urge a more orthodox living style on Muslims; national, or political, Islamism,

_____

[9]br_syed, "What is Islamic Extremism," *Sunni Forum* (June 22, 2006), http://www. sunniforum.com/forum/showthread.php?14932-what-is-islamic-extremism (accessed April 13, 2010).

[10]leo28, "What is Islamic Extremism," *Sunni Forum* (June 22, 2006), http://www.sunniforum .com/forum/showthread.php?14932-what-is-islamic-extremism (accessed April 13, 2010).

[11]sufisticated and tamiki, "What is Islamic Extremism," *Sunni Forum* (June 22, 2006), http://www. sunniforum.com/forum/showthread.php?14932-what-is-islamic-extremism (accessed April 13, 2010).

[12]Gvosdev and Takeyh, 4.

which is a political agenda for gaining power within in a Muslim nation and changing state policy to conform with *shari'a*; and global Islamism as practiced by *Al Qaeda*, which confronts the entire world as it attempts to unite Muslims by blaming Christian and Jewish powers and ignorant Muslim regimes for corrupting Islam.[13]

These three forms of Islamism mirror the factions of *Salafism*. *Salafi* is a term that in general refers to any orthodox Muslim, but in modern usage refers to Wahhabis and Islamists.[14] The term comes from the *Salaf*, who were the pious companions of the Prophet that collected the *hadith* and created the science of Islamic jurisprudence, laying the foundation for the body of law known as the *shari'a*.[15] *Salafi* strategy is based on the concept that Islam became decadent over time because followers strayed from the true path. Recapturing the glory of the time of the Prophet and the *ummah*, or Muslim community, requires a return to the "authentic" faith and practices of Muhammad and his companions and rejection of innovation. *Salafists* themselves debated whether to adopt the name because the word did not appear in the *Qur'an*.[16] Because *Salafism* revolves around applying religious beliefs to contemporary issues and problems, the subjective nature of doing so results in three major factions of *Salafists*, which are also

---

[13]Meghnad Desai, *Rethinking Islamism: The Ideology of the New Terror* (London: I.B.Tauris & Co. Ltd, 2007), 24-26, 96-97.

[14]"Those typically called *Wahhabis* reject the term because it suggests that they follow Ibn Wahhab, a person, rather than God. This, for conservative Muslims, would be tantamount to apostasy. They instead use the term *Salafi*." Quintan Wiktorowicz, "A Genealogy of Radical Islam," *Studies in Conflict & Terrorism* Vol. 28, No. 2 (2005): 94.

[15]Mary Habeck, *Knowing the Enemy: Jihadist Ideology and the War on Terror* (New Haven: Yale University Press, 2006), 43, 234, 236. *Hadith* (plural *ahadith*) are narrative records of traditions or sayings of the Prophet Muhammad.

[16]Quintan Wiktorowicz, "Anatomy of the *Salafi* Movement," *Studies in Conflict and Terrorism*, Vol. 29, No. 3. (May 2006): 219.

representative of the three major forms of Islamism outlined in the preceding paragraph: the purists, the politicos, and the *jihadis*.[17]

Purists are typically from the older generation and focus on nonviolent means to spread *Salafist* beliefs. They view the West as an eternal enemy that pollutes Islam with corrupt concepts and values. All *Salafists* believe the West wants to destroy Islam, but purists actively try to prevent any usage of Western values, behaviors, or systems of logic to discuss religion. Quintan Wiktorowicz, professor of International Studies at Rhodes College in Tennessee, notes, "although the purists are strongly anti-Western (and anti-American), they are also the least likely to support the use of violence."[18]

Purists do not view themselves as a political group, in contrast to the politicos who emphasize the application of the *Salafi* creed in politics. The politicos are of a younger generation and see themselves as better able to apply *Salafi* beliefs to a modern context. The politico movement began as members of the Egyptian Muslim Brotherhood fled to Saudi Arabia in the 1960s to avoid being jailed and/or executed by President Gamal Abd al-Nasser and, according to Wiktorowicz, brought with them "...a more politically oriented agenda and awareness to the predominantly purist Saudi context."[19] Although politicos are highly critical of incumbent regimes they typically stop short of revolution, unlike the *jihadis*.

---

[17]"Central to these divisions is a debate about which faction is best suited to interpret modern problems. To a large extent, this is a generational struggle between the senior purists, on the one hand, and the younger politico and jihadi scholars, on the other. The younger generation of more politically minded Salafis believes it has a better grasp of the complexities of contemporary politics and international affairs as well as intellectual autonomy. These scholars argue that this allows them to issue better informed, honest rulings. The purists, in contrast, emphasize their religious training and credentials and argue that an emphasis on politics and current affairs threatens to erode the purity of Islam by introducing temporal human emotions and desires." Quintan Wiktorowicz, "Anatomy of the *Salafi* Movement," *Studies in Conflict and Terrorism*, Vol. 29, No. 3. (May 2006): 208, 216-217.

[18]Ibid, 218, 234.

[19]Ibid, 208-222.

The contemporary faction of *Salafist jihadis* emerged during the 1979-1989 Soviet-Afghan War. A *jihadi* is one who fights out of a sense of moral and/or religious obligation. *Jihadis* often serve as the military arm of an Islamist organization, helping to carry out the Islamist vision. They do not distinguish between politics and warfare – for *jihadis* they are one and the same.[20] According to Marc Sageman, author of *Understanding Terror Networks*:

> The global *Salafi jihad* is a worldwide religious revivalist movement with the goal of reestablishing past Muslim glory in a great Islamic state... It preaches...the restoration of authentic Islam, and advocates a strategy of violent *jihad*, resulting in an explosion of terror to wipe out what it regards as local political heresy. The global version of this movement advocates the defeat of the Western powers that prevent the establishment of a true Islamist state.[21]

The Arabic word *mujahid* is literally one who struggles; the pluralized *mujahidin* identifies those who fight *jihad,* and it currently applies to the various *jihadi* groups in Afghanistan.

Who are the *Jihadists* in Afghanistan?

With a basic conception of relevant terms and an appreciation for the tension that results from the differences between Western and Muslim perspectives, one has a foundation for understanding the historical context of the *jihad* in Afghanistan. There are two major types of organizations fighting in Afghanistan – those with local objectives and those with global objectives. Afghanistan has historically been a tribal-based society with battles between warlords to gain territory or settle matters of honor. Three main groups emerged as a result of the 1979 Soviet invasion of Afghanistan: The Afghan Islamists and the Taliban both fought to take control of the government from the Soviet-backed regime, while the "Arab Afghans" fought for the purpose of *jihad* to defend a Muslim nation against an infidel enemy. Bin Laden and Azzam formed their conception of the organization that would become bin Laden's *Al Qaeda* in this setting of a *jihad* fought to expel the infidel Soviets from Muslim land. While the Society of

---

[20]Ibid, 221, 225.

[21]Marc Sageman, *Understanding Terror Networks* (Philadelphia: University of Pennsylvania Press, 2004), 1.

Muslim Brothers, more simply known as the Muslim Brotherhood, is covered in greater detail later, it is important to note the influence this Egyptian organization and its key thinkers had in shaping and influencing the ideology of those fighting in Afghanistan.

Afghan Islamists – Challengers to the Taliban for Control of Afghanistan

The Afghan Islamist movement, like so many opposition movements throughout the Middle East, emerged among the educated youth and was attributable in part to the education exchange between Cairo and Kabul in the 1960s. The Egyptian students who came to Kabul brought the ideology of the Muslim Brothers with them, and the young Afghanis could easily relate to the social and political injustices that inspired the Egyptian movement.[22] In 1965 students at Kabul University formed a Muslim Youth Organization known as the *ikhwan*.[23]

Burhanuddin Rabbani, a professor of jurisprudence at Kabul University, was the leader of the Afghan Islamists. Rabbani had close ties with senior Egyptian Muslim Brothers, and he was one of the first Afghans to translate Egyptian Islamist Sayyid Qutb's writings into Dari. The Islamists pursued a radical political ideology in order to bring about an Islamic revolution in Afghanistan. They wanted to create a true Islamic society inspired by the Prophet Muhammad, but one that would address the challenges of the modern world.[24]

---

[22]"The background of the Kabul Islamists is revealing. They were all from the provinces... Most were from relatively wealthy backgrounds... They were almost all university educated, mainly in technical faculties. Such men were also to provide the bulk of the 20 or 30 senior activists who joined bin Laden in Afghanistan after 1996, further evidencing the essentially political roots, and aims, of the 'al-Qaeda hardcore'...." Jason Burke, *Al-Qaeda: The True Story of Radical Islam* (London: I.B. Tauris & Co Ltd, 2006), 66.

[23]"*Ikhwan*," Encyclopedia Britannica online. http://www.britannica.com/EBchecked/topic/282606 /Ikhwan (acessed April 8, 2010). *Ikhwan* is an Arabic word meaning brethren. The original *Ikhwan* formed in Saudi Arabia in 1912 under Ibn Saud. Religious reformer and Islamic fundamentalist Ibn 'Abd al-Wahhab instructed the *Ikhwan*. Hassan al-Banna later adopted the name *ikhwan* for his own organization, the Society of Muslim Brothers.

[24]Ahmed Rashid, *Taliban: Militant Islam, Oil and Fundamentalism in Central Asia* (New Haven: Yale University Press, 2001), 19.

Before the Islamists carried out their revolutionary goal, Mohammed Daud Khan led a military coup to overthrow the king – his cousin – and established a pro-Soviet Republic in Kabul in 1973. The leaders of Khan's opposition – Rabbani, Gulbuddin Hekmatyar, and Ahmed Shah Masud, fled to Peshawar, where the Pakistani government gave them refuge under Inter-Services Intelligence Directorate (ISI) protection. The Islamists formed the basis for the *mujahidin* who fought the Soviets after their 1979 invasion of Afghanistan. Hekmatyar, Abdul Rasul Sayyaf and others built training camps in Pakistan with Saudi funds under the direction of the ISI. [25]

When the Soviets finally withdrew from Afghanistan in 1989, the Islamists became fractured in the resulting power void and split into various factions under leaders like Hekmatyar and Sayyaf. Afghanistan once again became divided into areas controlled by tribal warlords. The battle between these tribal factions for Kabul in the mid-1990s became a proxy conflict as Saudi Arabia and Pakistan supported the Taliban, and Iran, Russia, and India supported the Rabbani government. Pakistan provided training and equipment to the Afghan Islamists during the Soviet-Afghan War and tried unsuccessfully to form an anti-Rabbani alliance by uniting the warlords and the Taliban for the seizure of Kabul, but the Taliban refused to meet. The warlords then moved to defend Kabul in support of Rabbani.[26] The United States leaned toward the Taliban because of its anti-Iran foreign policy, but publicly denied support of either side.[27]

The Taliban – Extreme Fundamentalist *Salafi Jihadists* Claiming the Historical Right to Rule Afghanistan

The power struggle among *mujahidin* groups in the wake of the 1989 Soviet withdrawal and the fall of the regime in Kabul paved the way for Taliban ascendance.[28] Violence and

---

[25]Burke, 67.

[26]Rashid, 44-46.

[27]Ibid, 46-48.

[28]Bruce Riedel, *The Search for Al Qaeda: Its Leadership, Ideology, and Future* (Washington, D.C.: Brookings Institution Press, 2008), 64.

criminal activity became a means for *mujahidin* survival in the aftermath of the Soviet-Afghan War when external [US] support for the fighters suddenly stopped. Mullah Omar, joined by several students and Soviet War veterans, formed the Taliban in reaction to crimes the *mujahidin* were committing against the Afghan people. The Taliban's declared aims were to restore peace, disarm the population, enforce *shari'a* law, and defend the integrity and Islamic character of Afghanistan.[29]

As the Taliban restored order, they revived hopes among the Pashtun of renewed domination over Afghanistan. Most Taliban members were Pashtun, a fervently Sunni ethnic group that comprised forty percent of the Afghan population, and traced its roots back to the two eldest sons of Qais, a companion of the Prophet. Pashtuns had been the historical rulers of Afghanistan since the 18th century when tribal leader Ahmed Shah Durrani became "the father of the Afghan nation." The Durrani clan had ruled Afghanistan for more than 200 years, until Khan overthrew the king and declared Afghanistan a Republic in 1973.[30]

In the 1980s Pakistan saw the rise of Deobandism. The central focus of the Deobandi movement was the religious education provided in their *madrassas*. According to *Al-Qaeda* author Jason Burke, "The students at the *madrassas* [sic] were known as *taliban*, a Persianized plural of an Arabic word meaning seekers of knowledge or students."[31] The Deobandis ultimately established thousands of schools in the Pashtun region, and hundreds of thousands of boys and young men attended the Deobandi schools. The free education, along with room and board, offered by the schools attracted poor Afghan refugee children, as well as poor Pakistanis. Deobandi philosophy shuns innovation and stresses acceptance of old interpretations of the

---

[29]Rashid, 22.

[30]Ibid, 1, 10-11.

[31]Burke, 92- 93. Reference APPENDIX A for information about Deobandi beliefs and practices.

Qur'an and *hadith*, rather than forming modern interpretations to fit the times.[32] The Deobandis were the closest equivalent to Wahhabis in that region, so they received support and funding from governments and donors in the Gulf as part of the global effort to spread rigid *Salafi* strands of Islam.[33] Mullah Omar chose the name Taliban to indicate that his organization was a movement for purifying society.[34]

The Taliban seized control of Kabul in 1996 and immediately imposed a rigid form of *shari'a* law and strict religious values on Afghan society. The Northern Alliance formed in opposition to the new Taliban government.[35] Only Pakistan, Saudi Arabia, and the United Arab Emirates formally recognized the Taliban government; Russia, India, Iran, Tajikistan, and Uzbekistan backed the Northern Alliance.[36] The Taliban wanted to emulate the ideal Islamic society created by the Prophet Muhammad. For the country to be transformed to the pure origins of Islam, the *shari'a* had to be followed precisely. Under Taliban rule women could not work and had to remain in their homes at all times unless accompanied by a male relative, all girls' schools were closed, women had to be covered from head-to-toe, and men had to grow long beards. Taliban law also banned television, videos, satellite dishes, music, and games.[37] Some Muslim theologians questioned whether Taliban law was really an interpretation of *shari'a* or enforcement

---

[32]Roland Jacquard, *In the Name of Osama Bin Laden: Global Terrorism and the Bin Laden Brotherhood,* ed. Samia Serageldin, trans. George Holoch (London: Duke University Press, 2002), 38.

[33]Burke, 93.

[34]Rashid, 23.

[35]Burke, 118, 130. For the Taliban "...the source of much of the corruption that needed to be purged from Afghanistan was Kabul. The roots of this view lie in the profound gulf between the rulers and the ruled, the urban and the rural, that has developed over centuries in Afghanistan and underlies so many of the country's problems."

[36]Rohan Gunaratna, *Inside Al Qaeda: Global Network of Terror* (New York: Berkley Books, 2003), 53.

[37]Rashid, 50.

of their own tribal code of behavior, known as *Pashtunwali*.[38] According to Pakistani journalist

and *Taliban* author Ahmed Rashid:

> The Taliban's brand of Islamic fundamentalism was so extreme that it appeared
> to denigrate Islam's message of peace and tolerance and its capacity to live with
> other religious and ethnic groups. They were to inspire a new extremist form of
> fundamentalism across Pakistan and Central Asia, which refused to compromise
> with traditional Islamic values, social structures or existing state systems.[39]

The boys and young men who joined the Taliban in the 1990s were educated in Deobandi or

Taliban *madrassas* and had not known an Afghanistan without war. They had no jobs, no home

or family, no sense of future – all they could hold on to that gave their lives meaning was their

belief in a puritan Islam.[40] By 1999 the Taliban controlled more than eighty percent of

Afghanistan.[41]

Arab Afghans – Forerunners of *Al Qaeda*

The name "Arab Afghans" is misleading because none of the men in this group were

Afghani and many were not Arab. Arab Afghan was the common name used by both Muslims

and Westerners for the men who travelled to Afghanistan from other Muslim countries – like

---

[38]"This is an unwritten code controlling, guiding and balancing, to large extent, the form, character and discipline of the [Pashtun] way of life. ...It is framed on the principle of equality and retaliation ... deeply ingrained in the social structure of a [Pashtu's] life and is highly esteemed and held sacrosanct by all persons irrespective of their financial or social status. The more one adheres to its maxims, the more esteem he enjoys in his brotherhood and community... It is a concept conveying the meaning of [a] tribal socio-economic, political and cultural system in totality---courage, hospitality, kinship, loyalty, love for friends, hostility with enemy, chastity, morality, respecting rights... This code requires an Afghan to defend his motherland, to grant asylum to fugitives irrespective of their creed or caste, to take revenge... to offer protection, even to his deadly enemy, and wipe out insult with insult... At the same time these traits are true reflections of Islam but since [Pashtu] claim their origin well before the advent of Islam, it can safely be surmised that the [Pashtun] is a Muslim by virtue of his very blood. He is Muslim first and Muslim last... His ego is satisfied only when he kills his wife or sister charged with *tor* (illicit sexual relations) for, in this way, he considers himself relieved of disgrace and shame amongst his fellow-beings." Speenghar Zazai, "Pakhtunwali,"Afghan.net, http://www.afghanan.net/ pashto/pashtunwali/pashtunwali.htm (accessed April 11, 2010).

[39]Rashid, 2, 4.

[40]Ibid, 32.

[41]Burke, 130.

Egypt, Yemen, Saudi Arabia, and Chechnya – to join the *jihad*. Osama bin Laden was one of these men, and many of the Arab Afghan *mujahidin* stayed with bin Laden and became part of his *Al Qaeda* organization. Many also returned to their homes with the skills they learned in battle and a new ideology of *jihad* to start their own Islamic militant groups in countries around the world. It is important to note the setting for bin Laden's creation of *Al Qaeda*, because it provides insight into his reasoning for later attacks.

Bin Laden's *Jihadist* Ideology – Why the United States Should Care

> The first duty of the Islamic world is to exalt the word of *Allah* until it is
> supreme. Hence the only proper relationship to the non-Islamic world is of
> perpetual warfare... until the whole world is converted or submits to Islam.
> - Ann K.S. Lambton, *State and Community in Medieval Islam*

The *jihad* against a foreign invader – the Soviet Union – was a powerful rallying cry that united Muslims from all over the world for a common purpose, and bin Laden would apply this same reasoning when America became his target and the focus of his *jihadist* ideology. Several sources agree that the original *Al Qaeda*, an Arabic word meaning "base," was really just a database containing the personal information of the *mujahidin*.[42] *Al Qaeda* started to form in the mid-1980s around the Peshawar region of Pakistan, as young Muslims flocked to Pakistan and Afghanistan to participate in the Afghan *jihad*. Bin Laden developed his organization along the steps laid out by Sayyid Qutb's *Milestones*, steps that represented the way the Prophet Muhammad achieved his ideal Islamic society.

Initially the group called *Al Qaeda* consisted of a core of mainly Egyptian fighters with bin Laden as their leader.[43] His fighters swore an oath of allegiance to him, and they lived and trained in camps apart from other *jihadis*. Bin Laden continued to recruit fighters and grow his force. The group became the first global terrorist organization in history – breaking from the

---

[42]Ibid, 5-6.

[43]Burke, 85.

tradition of internally-focused, nationalist activists, and emerging as a community of Islamic *jihadists* fighting for Allah, for an ideology, and for an ideal Muslim society. Bin Laden had a larger vision to reunite the *ummah* – the Islamic community – and restore the caliphate, which was a symbol of unity and Muslim identity before it ended, in bin Laden's perception, as a result of Western influence.[44] According to author Jason Burke, "The ultimate goal [of *Al Qaeda*] is to drive the United States from the Muslim world (the *ummah*), destroy Israel, and create a *jihadist* caliphate along the lines of the Ottoman Empire at its height."[45]

In the mid-1990s bin Laden focused his ideology on expelling the West from the Muslim world. He believed achievement of this aim would unite the various Muslim factions, and then together they could return the Muslim world to its intended state - the caliphate.[46] *Al Qaeda* executed the 9/11 attacks to provoke the United States to invade Muslim lands, so they could achieve a decisive victory and gain support for the *jihad*. According to former CIA agent and author Bruce Riedel, *Al Qaeda* believed defeating US forces in Afghanistan "...would so undermine morale that America would withdraw from the Islamic world and retreat to an isolationist posture, leaving its corrupt allies in the Muslim world without a protector and at the mercy of the armies of *jihad*."[47] Bin Laden issued a rallying call to the *ummah* in October 2001,

---

[44]David Bukay, *From Muhammad to Bin Laden: Religious and Ideological Sources of the Homicide Bombers Phenomenon* (New Brunswick, New Jersey: Transaction Publishers, 2008), 281.

[45]"Since the abolition of the Ottoman Caliphate, no country has replaced Turkey as the Muslim world's center. According to Sayyid Qutb, in order to bring about a new Caliphate governed by God's law there must be a revival in one Muslim country, enabling it to attain that status. When the Taliban captured Kabul in 1996, Afghanistan became an official Islamic state, or emirate, ruled by *sharia*, and in the view of bin Laden and others, the strongest candidate for a new Caliphate." Bruce Lawrence, ed., *Messages to the World: The Statements of Osama Bin Laden,* trans. James Howarth (London: Verso, 2005), 42; Bruce Riedel, *The Search for Al Qaeda: Its Leadership, Ideology, and Future* (Washington, D.C.: Brookings Institution Press, 2008), 11.

[46]Burke, 165

[47]Habeck, 14; Bruce Riedel, *The Search for Al Qaeda: Its Leadership, Ideology, and Future* (Washington, D.C.: Brookings Institution Press, 2008), 33.

attempting to recreate the support he saw during the Soviet-Afghan War when *jihadists* from

around the world flocked to Afghanistan to defeat a common enemy:

> ...our concern is that our *ummah* unites...and that this nation should establish the righteous caliphate... The *ummah* is asked to unite itself in the face of this Crusaders' campaign, the strongest, most powerful, and most ferocious Crusaders' campaign to fall on the Islamic *ummah* since the dawn of Islamic history.[48]

Bin Laden has been clear about his intentions and goals from the beginning. It is vital to

understand his strategic aims and how those aims are supported by historical Islamic tradition.

Bin Laden uses this historical narrative and the endorsement of contemporary religious clerics to

rationalize and justify *Al Qaeda's* actions and rally support for his *jihad*. The current strategy of

Al Qaeda centers on three main objectives. The first is to conduct a protracted "bleeding" war

against the United States and its Western allies in Iraq and Afghanistan to effect a defeat like the

Soviet Union experienced in Afghanistan. Their second objective is to create a safe haven in

Pakistan for an operational headquarters, while creating new "franchises" throughout the Muslim

world to fight the West in those areas and overthrow pro-American regimes. Finally *Al Qaeda*

aims to build an infrastructure of supporters in the West, especially in Europe, to conduct attacks

and spread fear in the Western world. This approach could someday include employment of a

nuclear weapon or other weapon of mass destruction (WMD).[49] *Al Qaeda* achieved the latter two

goals and has had some success in achieving the first: The conflict in Afghanistan continues, and

while *Al Qaeda* has not defeated US and NATO forces, the US President's timeline to withdraw

troops from Afghanistan beginning in 2011 is no secret.[50] *Jihadis* in Afghanistan and Pakistan

only have to bide their time and then claim victory when the Western invaders are gone. The

---

[48]Lawrence, 121.

[49]Riedel, 11, 121-122, 133. Pakistan has roughly 200 nuclear weapons and is the most likely source for *Al Qaeda* to acquire such a device. *Al Qaeda's* highest priority targets for a nuclear attack are Israel followed by the United States.

[50]Barack Obama (Presidential Address to the Nation on the Way Forward in Afghanistan and Pakistan, United States Military Academy at West Point, West Point, NY, December 01, 2009).

withdrawal of US troops from Afghanistan while *Al Qaeda* remains undefeated plays into bin Laden's ideological goals. Bin Laden made clear his objectives and *Al Qaeda* has conducted operations in support of them, so it would be a logical conclusion that attainment of a nuclear weapon or WMD is not just a whim, but an actual goal, and that *Al Qaeda* is applying effort toward that end. To understand the ideology driving *Al Qaeda's* operations, one should begin by exploring the historical foundations of Islam and the *Salafi* theorists and activists responsible for inspiring bin Laden.

Roots of Bin Laden's *Jihadist* Ideology

By tracing the history of *Al Qaeda's* ideological concepts, one gains a clearer understanding of how bin Laden and Zawahiri have been able to entice disenchanted Muslims to join a *jihad* designed to overthrow apostate governments, abolish the corrupting influences of modernity and Westernization to create an ideal society governed by *shari'a* law, and restore the Islamic caliphate. Bin Laden took a number of themes in the Muslim discourse about modernity and turned them into a global ideology.[51] One can trace the basis for bin Laden's ideology back to the Prophet Muhammad, and understanding the key Islamic concepts that legitimize *Al Qaeda's* actions for some in the Muslim world is necessary in order to develop ways to counter that line of thought. According to *Christian Science Monitor* reporter Robert Marquand, bin Laden promotes the concept that a person's "...credentials as a *true Muslim* are increasingly based on a willingness to use violence."[52] Numerous Islamic scholars have written about the ideal Islamic society of the past and the steps to be taken in order to achieve a more authentic Islamic state in the present. Another aspect that connects these Islamists is the premise that someone else

---

[51]Meghnad Desai, *Rethinking Islamism: The Ideology of the New Terror* (London: I.B.Tauris & Co. Ltd, 2007), 95.

[52]Robert Marquand, "The Tenets of Terror," *The Christian Science Monitor* , csmonitor.com (October 18, 2001), http://www.csmonitor.com/2001/1018/p1s2-wogi.html (accessed December 6, 2009).

is to blame for the decayed or corrupted state of society, and the blame is usually placed on an ignorant Muslim regime or on the Christian-Jewish alliance. The Islamists highlighted in this paper have most influenced bin Laden's thoughts and the formation of his ideology. Bin Laden was raised and educated in the Wahhabist culture of Saudi Arabia. He has referenced the words of Ibn Taymiyya and Sayyid Qutb in his own writing and speeches, and his mentors have also been influenced by the works of the *Salafists* presented here.

Back to the Beginning: The Roots of *Jihad* – Muhammad, The Prophet (570-632 AD)

Current-day Islamic *jihadists* still refer to Muhammad's use of violence to justify their own actions. Muhammad biographer Richard Gabriel said, "Muhammad's unshakable belief in Islam... revolutionized warfare in Arabia... and created the first army in the ancient world motivated by a coherent system of ideological belief."[53] Muhammad fought to bring about a new social order based on Islam. He formed his army around a core of loyal cadre – an inner circle – who advised him as well as helped to recruit and organize his forces. Muhammad then established a base from which he could conduct military operations.[54] In addition to his core cadre, Muhammad formed a secret group of his most devoted and pious followers. This group, called the *suffah*, protected the Prophet and acted as a kind of "secret police" that would do whatever mission he gave them, including assassination and acts of terror. Muhammad understood the necessity of the population's support in order to achieve his vision of a truly Islamic society, and he used propaganda to spread his message among the people and create a community of believers – the original *ummah*.[55] Under this new form of ideological warfare,

---

[53]Richard A. Gabriel, *Muhammad: Islam's First Great General* (Norman: University of Oklahoma Press, 2007), xix.

[54]Ibid, xxii. Muhammad chose Medina as his base. Operations were mostly raids and ambushes aimed at isolating Mecca, the main city of Muhammad's opposition.

[55]Ibid, xxv-xxvi.

Muhammad promoted the idea that it was every Muslim's obligation to fight in defense of Islam, and it was this ideology that attracted fighters to his cause. These steps Muhammad took toward arriving at a true Islamic society – forming an elite inner circle, establishing a base apart from society, using propaganda to gain popular support and grow his group of followers – appear in the writings of Sayyid Qutb and mirror the way bin Laden formed *Al Qaeda*.

Pre-Modern *Salafist* with Modern-Day Influence – Ibn Taymiyya (1263-1328 AD)

Ibn Taymiyya believed the ideal Muslim community was Muhammad's original community in Medina.[56] Taymiyya saw the Muslim world of his time in a state of decline, losing its sense of morality and purity, in the years after Muhammad's death. He formed his perception of a weakened Muslim world in the wake of the Christian Crusades and the Mongol capture of Baghdad - then seat of the caliphate. Taymiyya thought the only way to restore a pure Islamic society was to return to the way of life prescribed in the *Qur'an* and *sunna*.[57] The Mongols at one point imprisoned Taymiyya for heresy for continuing to promote his *Salafist* beliefs despite opposition from state and religious leaders.[58] He challenged the Mongol rulers who, despite having converted to Islam, did not uphold *shari'a* law. According to Taymiyya biographer Austin Cline, "Ibn Taymiyya issued a *fatwa* against [the ruling Mongols], thus starting a new precedent

---

[56]Austin Cline, "Ibn Taymiyyah: Profile and Biography," About.com - Agnosticism/Atheism, http://atheism.about.com/library/FAQs/islam/blfaq_islam_taymiyyah.htm (accessed 6 December 2009).

[57]"Also spelled *Sunnah*. (Arabic: "habitual practice"), the body of traditional social and legal custom and practice of the Muslim community. In pre-Islāmic Arabia, *sunna* referred to precedents established by tribal ancestors, accepted as normative, and practiced by the entire community." "*sunna*," Encyclopædia Britannica, 2009, Encyclopædia Britannica Online, http://www.britannica.com/EBchecked/topic/573993/*sunna* (accessed 6 December 2009); James Pavlin, "Ibn Taymiyya, Taqi al-Din (1263-1328)," Islamic Philosophy Online, http://www.muslimphilosophy. com/ip/rep/H039.htm (accessed 6 December 2009).

[58]Quintan Wiktorowicz, "Anatomy of the *Salafi* Movement," *Studies in Conflict & Terrorism* 29 (2006): 207-239.

of treating... apostates as worthy of violent revolution, even if they are political leaders."[59] The writings and ideas of Ibn Taymiyya continue to inspire modern-day *Salafists*, from the Wahabbis to the Muslim Brotherhood to Osama bin Laden, all of whom see Taymiyya as a man of righteous conviction willing to sacrifice himself for his beliefs and who continue to promote the concept that it is the duty of Muslims to revolt against corrupt and untrue leaders, including Muslim leaders, in order to establish a more authentic Islamic state.[60]

Founder of *Salafi* Fundamentalism – Muhammad 'Abd al-Wahhab (1703-1792) and the *Ikhwan*

Bin Laden's ideology is truly rooted in Saudi Arabia and emerges from the Wahhabi-guided *Ikhwan* movement. Identifying the source of opposition provides insight into why bin Laden thinks and acts as he does. Muhammad Abd al-Wahhab established the Islamic movement of Wahhabism based on his particular interpretation of Islamic doctrine, which envisions an Islamic empire ruled by strict puritanical Islamic law. Followers of Wahhab's teachings refer to themselves as *Salafis*, not Wahhabis, because the term Wahhabi infers that they follow a person instead of worshipping god.[61] In his early 20s, Wahhab studied in Medina, to include studying the works of Ibn Taymiyya. Wahhab moved to Dir'iyya around 1735 and formed an alliance with Muhammad ibn Saud, the founder of the Saudi dynasty. With Saud's support, Wahhab declared *jihad* against all who did not share his understanding of *tawhid* – the oneness of Allah, monotheism.[62] Some compare Wahhab's conviction and actions to those of the Kharijites.[63]

---

[59]Austin Cline, "Ibn Taymiyyah: Profile and Biography," About.com - Agnosticism/Atheism, http://atheism.about.com/library/FAQs/islam/blfaq_islam_taymiyyah.htm (accessed 6 December 2009).

[60]Quintan Wiktorowicz, "Anatomy of the *Salafi* Movement," *Studies in Conflict & Terrorism* 29 (2006): 207-239; Habeck, 22.

[61]Quintan Wiktorowicz, "A Genealogy of Radical Islam," *Studies in Conflict & Terrorism* 28 (2005): 94.

[62]Habeck, 23-24.

[63]Hamid Algar, *Wahhabism: A Critical Essay* (Oneonta, New York: Islamic Publications International, 2002), 21. See APPENDIX B for further information about the Kharijites.

Even after the death of ibn Saud in 1765 and the death of Wahhab in 1792 the alliance remained intact. The *Ikhwan* – meaning Brothers or Brotherhood – the martial arm of Wahhabism, continued to fight their *jihad* against nonbelievers while expanding the House of Saud. The Saud family allowed the strict Wahhabi interpretation of Islam to be incorporated in Saudi society.[64]

The Saud family funded the exportation of Wahhabism, in part as a measure to keep the Wahabbis in check as oil wealth brought increasing luxury and Western influence to the nation and expanded the rift between tradition and modernity in Saudi Arabia. The Wahhabi clerics eventually developed a strong anti-American and anti-Western view because they believed this Western influence contributed to the corruption of Saudi society. Because of the royal family's increased dealings with the West, the *Ikhwan* revolted against the Saudi government in 1927-28. The government crushed the revolution attempt, but many of the radical *Ikhwan* relocated to Egypt following the rebellion.[65]

From Saudi Arabia to Egypt: the Emergence of Political Islam – Hassan al-Banna (1906-1949) and the Society of Muslim Brothers

Hassan al-Banna arrived in Cairo to complete his education as a teacher in the 1920s. During this period the Muslim world reeled in the wake of the 1924 Turkish revolution that brought an end to the last Islamic caliphate, the formation of the British Mandate for Palestine – a precursor to the state of Israel, and the resettlement of the radical *Ikhwan* from Saudi Arabia into a newly independent Egyptian society. Banna had a history of activism from his youth, becoming

---

[64]"...promoting Wahhabism was an asset to [the government] in forging cohesion among the tribal peoples and districts of the peninsula. By reviving the notion of a community of believers, united by their submission to God, Wahhabism helped to forge a sense of common identity that was to supersede parochial loyalties... [The Saudi king] undercut traditional hierarchies of power and made devotion to Islam and to himself as the rightly guided Islamic ruler the glue that would hold his kingdom together... Unity in Islam of the Muslim *ummah* under Al Saud leadership was the basis for the legitimacy of the Saudi state." "Wahhabi Theology," Saudi Arabia, Helen Chapin Metz, ed., *Saudi Arabia: A Country Study* (Washington: GPO for the Library of Congress, 1992), http://countrystudies.us/saudi-arabia/27.htm (accessed 19 March 2010).

[65]"Muslim Brotherhood: The Roots of the Pan-Islamic *Jihad*," Tell Children the Truth, http://www. tellthechildrenthetruth.com/mbhood_en.html (accessed 6 December 2009).

the leader of the Society for Moral Behavior at the age of 12, and then forming the Society for the Prevention of the Forbidden with some of his classmates. According to *Al-Qaeda* author Jason Burke, Banna "...saw Islam as a perfect, total and all-encompassing system, regulating every part of the social, political, personal and religious life of the believer."[66] When he saw the growing gap between traditional religious devotion and secularist movements that weakened religion, he formed a group of students who preached the true Islamic faith to the people all over Egypt. The group became formalized in 1928 with the establishment of the Society of Muslim Brothers, simply known as the Muslim Brotherhood. The Society held the view that the "enemies of Islam" destroyed the Islamic state and allowed imperialists to take over the Muslim world. In order to achieve revival of the Islamic nation, Muslims had to take steps toward liberation of Muslim states, which would lead to unification of the Arab world under a *shari'a*-ruled caliphate.[67] An ideology emerged based on: Islam as a total system, complete unto itself; an Islam formulated from and based on its two primary sources, the *Qur'an* and the *Sunna* – reminiscent of Ibn Taymiyya's philosophy; and an Islam applicable to all times and all places.[68]

The nature of the Muslim Brothers was initially passive, as the group spread its ideas through propaganda, education, and social programs, much like the Prophet had in the early days of Islam.[69] At a conference in 1935 the Brothers adopted the membership classification degrees of assistant, related, active, and struggler, or *mujahid*. Banna considered strugglers to be the most dedicated and active members who would serve God and the message.[70] A "secret apparatus,"

---

[66]Burke, 48.

[67]Richard S. Mitchell, *The Society of the Muslim Brothers* (New York: Oxford University Press, 1993), 269.

[68]Mitchell, 14.

[69]Gabriel, xxvi.

[70]"These organizational developments corresponded in time with the beginning of the Brothers' concern for, and activity in, Palestine – the issue which, with the British occupation, was the most notably identified by the members themselves with the inspiration for political activism in the Society." Mitchell, 31.

reminiscent of the Prophet's *suffah* formed within the Muslim Brothers. Mitchell, noted for his study of the Muslim Brothers, described the secret wing: "Inspired... by the concept of *jihad*, formalized into an organization under the pressures of nationalist agitation, the secret apparatus was almost immediately rationalized as an instrument for the defense of Islam and the Society."[71] Banna considered the group to be an army of liberation.[72] According to Mitchell, "If the Muslim Brothers were more effectively violent than other groups... it was because *militancy* and *martyrdom* had been elevated to central virtues in the Society's ethos."[73] Much like the Wahhabis, the Muslim Brothers movement compares historically to that of the Kharijites, a group that pursued violence against unbelievers and apostates for not living up to the standards of authentic Islam.[74]

A more militant version of the Muslim Brothers emerged in the 1940s. Members of the Society formed ties with the Free Officers, a group of Egyptian Army officers planning revolution; two of the army officers who had meetings with the Brothers were Anwar al-Sadat and Gamal Abd al-Nasser, both of whom would later become president of Egypt. The Muslim Brothers mobilized in 1947-1948 for *jihad* during the Palestine War, fighting alongside the Egyptian Army. In December 1948 the Egyptian government ordered the dissolution of the Society because of suspicion the Brothers were planning a revolution. In February 1949 a group of army officers backed by the Egyptian government assassinated Banna.[75]

The Society remained active even after the death of its founder and leader. In late 1950 Egyptian King Faruq believed thirty-three percent of his army officers were part of the Muslim

---

[71]Ibid, 32.

[72]Ibid, 207. Banna told the members repeatedly that they were "the troops of God" shielded by their "Islamic morality."

[73]Ibid, 206.

[74]Ibid, 320. The Egyptian government charged the Society with being *Khawarij* in 1948 and again in 1954, both periods when the government perceived a revolutionary threat from the organization.

[75]Ibid, 65, 71.

Brothers.[76] The Muslim Brothers maintained a connection with the Free Officers movement and assisted them in carrying out the 1952 coup that overthrew the king. Following the revolution, the Brothers urged the new government to establish rule of law on the basis of Islam and *shari'a*.[77] Around the time Sayyid Qutb joined the Muslim Brothers, a schism within the Society divided the group along political-religious and activist lines. The secret apparatus became more active, despite the protests of the political members who sought to have the group abolished.

Godfather Ideologue of *Al Qaeda* – Sayyid Qutb (1906-1965)

Sayyid Qutb, like Ibn Taymiyya and Wahhab, viewed the period of Muhammad as a "period of pristine Islam" – the Muslim ideal.[78] Also like Ibn Taymiyya, Qutb justified *jihad* against apostate rulers. Qutb based a society's Islamic-ness not on whether it maintained a majority of Muslims but on whether it followed the *shari'a*. For Qutb *shari'a* law was the only measure to determine whether a society was authentically Islamic.[79] Qutb saw Islam as more than religion, but a way of life that one could not separate from everyday decisions and actions.[80]

In the 1920s the Middle East saw increased Western influence with the dissolution of the last Caliphate in Turkey and the British Mandate for Palestine, even as many countries – including Egypt – gained independence from colonial rule. Qutb's writing began to take on a more anti-Western slant in the 1930s. Qutb believed the Egyptian government looked for Western solutions to its social problems even though, fundamentally, the ideals of the West were incompatible with Islam.[81] In 1946 he spoke out against the United States because of President

---

[76]Ibid, 100.

[77]Ibid, 101-107.

[78]Musallam, 71.

[79]Habeck, 64.

[80]Sayyid Qutb, *Social Justice In Islam,* trans. John. B. Hardie, revised edition (Oneonta, NY: Islamic Publications International, 2000), 20.

[81]Ibid.

Truman's support of Jewish immigration to Palestine. His anti-American feelings solidified during his1948-1950 visit to the United States, where he viewed Americans as hurried, greedy, lustful, and shallow.[82]

While Qutb was aware of the Muslim Brothers in Egypt, he was not originally a fan of any of the Islamic political groups of the time, believing they were too weak to restore a decayed society. When he saw the jubilant American reaction to news of Banna's death in 1949, Qutb realized the threat al-Banna had posed to the West, and his negative feelings about the Muslim Brothers changed. He joined the Society in 1953 and became head of the organization's Propagation of the Message section.[83]

In 1954 the secret apparatus of the Muslim Brothers devised a plan to assassinate Nasser. Their attempt failed and ultimately turned the public against the Brotherhood. While Qutb was not charged for any involvement in the assassination plot, the government arrested and imprisoned him from 1954-1964 for "anti-government agitation." Qutb's thinking became more radical during his time in prison. According to Qutb biographer Adnan Musallam, "Despite censorship, Qutb managed to write many works that would eventually make him the leading ideologue of radical and *jihad*ist Islamists."[84] His most controversial work, *Milestones*, calls for establishment of a true Islamic society and overthrow through *jihad* of existing regimes. The book's title reflected Qutb's idea of steps or intermediate goals that lead to achievement of the final objective – the ideal Islamic state –mirroring the steps taken by Muhammad and resembling bin Laden's development of *Al Qaeda* to carry out his ideological aims. In his book *Overcoming Tradition and Modernity*, Robert D. Lee outlines the program Qutb proposed for moving a Muslim society to a state of Islam:

---

[82]Musallam, 86, 114.

[83]Ibid, 93, 113, 121, 136.

[84]Ibid, 150-151.

(1) recruitment of a vanguard elite, (2) solidification of a group consciousness, (3) segregation of the group from society, (4) enlargement of the group, (5) seizure of power, and (6) establishment of the new society.[85]

Qutb's vanguard apparatus indicated a split from the Muslim Brothers' political movement and, according to Qutb biographer Sharif Yunis, marked "...the moment of the ideological foundation of radical political Islam."[86] *Milestones* ultimately became the focus of Qutb's 1966 arrest and trial, resulting in his execution for plotting to overthrow Nasser's regime.

Musallam said, "Qutb's writings comprise extreme hostility toward the West, insistence on establishing a *Shari'a*-based society, the overthrow of governments not ruled by *Shari'a* through *jihad*, hatred of Jews, and distrust of Christians."[87] His writings are a "manifesto" for the "revolutionary Islamists" who joined the war against the Soviets in 1979-1980 in Afghanistan, those same Islamists who went on to create *Al Qaeda*. Many have dubbed Qutb "...the godfather ideologue of Osama bin Laden, Ayman al-Zawahiri, and *al-Qaeda*."[88] In 2001 Zawahiri said, "Sayyid Qutb's call for loyalty to God's oneness and to acknowledge God's sole authority and sovereignty was the spark that ignited the Islamic revolution against the enemies of Islam at home and abroad. The bloody chapters of this revolution continue to unfold day after day."[89]

The Muslim Brotherhood today has reverted to its original method of political activism and winning support of the population through social programs while denouncing the violent actions of *jihadist* organizations like *Al Qaeda*. The Brotherhood has attempted to neutralize American opposition by trying to persuade outsiders the group is a moderate Islamist movement in order to pave the way for future assumption of political power in Egypt. However, the

---

[85]Robert D. Lee, *Overcoming Tradition and Modernity: The Search for Islamic Authenticity* (Boulder: Westview Press, 1997), 104.

[86]Musallam, 155.

[87]Ibid, 194.

[88]Ibid, viii, 172.

[89]Ibid, 167.

organization's leaders have remained unwilling to make any ideological concessions in order to open a dialogue with the United States and have stated the purpose of such dialogue would be to demand that the West respect the right of Muslims to choose their way of life to be ruled by *shari'a*.[90]

From the Roots of *Jihad* to the Seeds of *Al Qaeda*: Past Meets Present – Dr. Abdullah Azzam (1941-1989)

Dr. Abdullah Azzam became the link between the ideas of the past and the ideology of present-day *jihadist* groups, particularly *Al Qaeda*. Central to Azzam's writings is the idea that *jihad* is an eternal activity that must never cease.[91] He was friendly with the family of Qutb and a devout student of Sayyid Qutb's thought.[92] Azzam, like Qutb, was greatly influenced by Ibn Taymiyya's writing, and he pointed to Taymiyyah's *fatwa* against the Crusaders and Mongols as justification that *jihad* is an obligation and the moral responsibility of every Muslim.[93] He emphasized the religious obligation to conduct *jihad* against Western invaders, quoting Ibn Taymiyya, "As for the occupying enemy who corrupts religion and life, nothing is more urgent after faith than repelling him."[94] In his writings Azzam also referenced Qutb's idea of a "vanguard" of the most committed fighters who would carry forward the banner of Islam and

---

[90]Israel Elad Altman, "The Crisis of the Arab Brotherhood," *Current Trends in Islamist Ideology*, Volume 6 (November 29, 2007), Hudson Institute: Center on Islam, Democracy, and the Future of the Muslim World, http://www.currenttrends.org/research/detail/the-crisis-of-the-arab-brotherhood (accessed August 6, 2009).

[91]Gilles Kepel and Jean-Pierre Milelli, eds., *Al Qaeda in its Own Words,* trans. Pascale Ghazaleh (Cambridge, Mass.: Belknap Press of Harvard University Press, 2008), 115-116, 303.

[92]Musallam, 190.

[93]Youssef Aboul-Enein, LCDR, MSC, USN, "The Late Sheikh Abdullah Azzam's Books," The Combatting Terrorism Center, http://ctc.usma.edu/publications/publications.asp (accessed 24 November 2009).

[94]Kepel and Milelli, 117.

bring the Muslim world nearer to its ideal Islamic society.[95]

In the first of his three-part commentary on Azzam's books, United States Navy

Lieutenant Commander Youssef Aboul-Enein compares Azzam's influence on *Al Qaeda* to that

of Carl von Clausewitz for conventional military forces.[96] According to Aboul-Enein:

> Sheikh Abdullah Azzam, more than any other cleric, is considered the strategic
> founder of *Al Qaeda*. His very utterances of the need to establish an *al-Qaida
> al-Sulba* (firm foundation) to export *jihad* where Muslims are persecuted is the
> name Bin Laden finally settled on when naming his organization *Al Qaeda*.[97]

Azzam was Palestinian and had been a member of the Muslim Brothers since 1959.[98] The Israeli-

Palestinian issue helped frame his ideology and worldview – his family relocated to a refugee

camp in Jordan after the 1967 Arab-Israeli War.[99] Azzam moved to Peshawar, Pakistan, in 1984

to recruit and organize *jihadis* for the war in Afghanistan along with his former student, Osama

bin Laden. In many places his recruiting efforts were handled through the existing Muslim

Brothers structure. Azzam was a key figure in urging the idea of martyrdom through suicide

operations on new recruits.[100]

---

[95]"Every principle needs a vanguard to carry it forward and [to] put up with heavy tasks and enormous sacrifices. There is no ideology, neither earthly nor heavenly, that does not require ... a vanguard that gives everything it possesses in order to achieve victory ... It carries the flag all along the sheer, endless and difficult path until it reaches its destination in the reality of life, since Allah has destined that it should make it and manifest itself. This vanguard constitutes the strong foundation (*al-qaeda al-sulbah*) for the expected society." Jason Burke, *Al-Qaeda: The True Story of Radical Islam* (London: I.B. Tauris & Co Ltd, 2006), 2-3.

[96]Youssef Aboul-Enein, LCDR, MSC, USN, "The Late Sheikh Abdullah Azzam's Books," The Combatting Terrorism Center, http://ctc.usma.edu/publications/publications.asp (accessed 24 November 2009).

[97]Ibid.

[98]Burke, 72.

[99]Gilles Kepel and Jean-Pierre Milelli, eds., *Al Qaeda in its Own Words,* trans. Pascale Ghazaleh (Cambridge, Mass.: Belknap Press of Harvard University Press, 2008), 85.

[100]Burke, 73-75.

Who Is Really in Charge of *Al Qaeda*? – Dr. Ayman al-Zawahiri (1951-   ) and Egyptian Islamic *Jihad*

Dr. Ayman al-Zawahiri, like those mentioned in the previous paragraphs, sought a return to a pure Islamic society; but unlike the other Islamists, Zawahiri did not look back to the time of Muhammad for his model. Zawahiri's ideology focused on what he perceived as the decline of the Islamic world beginning in 1924 with the fall of the last caliphate. Zawahiri blamed the caliphate's downfall on a conspiracy between the West and the Zionists to create a Jewish state in Palestine. According to author Bruce Riedel, "No tragedy is as powerful in [Zawahiri's] history of Islam as the loss of Palestine to the Zionists."[101]

Zawahiri was born and raised in Cairo, and he was greatly affected by Sayyid Qutb's life and death. Qutb's writing provided the foundation for Zawahiri's political ideology.[102] Zawahiri began his career as a revolutionary at the age of 15, following Qutb's execution, when he organized a group of students to study the writing of Qutb and make plans to overthrow the Nasser government and create an Islamic state.[103] His followers came to be known as the Islamic *Jihad*.

Zawahiri graduated from medical school in 1974, and by 1978, after serving three years as a surgeon in the Egyptian army, practiced medicine in clinics sponsored by the Muslim Brothers. In 1980 he travelled to Peshawar to provide humanitarian assistance to the Afghan refugees, and it is possible he first met bin Laden in Pakistan during that time. Zawahiri was back in Cairo when President Sadat was assassinated in 1981. While the Islamic *Jihad* was still plotting to overthrow the government, the cell was not directly involved in the murder. Despite that, Zawahiri was arrested and jailed along with thousands of others. According to author Bruce

---

[101]Riedel, 25.

[102]Stephanie Lacroix, "Ayman al-Zawahiri, Veteran of Jihad," In *Al Qaeda in its Own Words*, Gilles Kepel and Jean-Pierre Milelli, eds., trans. Pascale Ghazaleh (Cambridge, Mass.: Belknap Press of Harvard University Press, 2008), 150.

[103]Riedel, 18.

Riedel, this was the "defining moment" in Zawahiri's life: "It transformed him from an agitator and critic of the Egyptian government to a spokesman for revolutionary violence...."[104]

Following his release from prison, Zawahiri fled to Saudi Arabia where he again met up with bin Laden. The two travelled in and out of Pakistan in the 1980s and 1990s and assisted the Afghanistan *mujahidin*, together with Azzam. They relocated to Sudan in 1994. Zawahiri influenced bin Laden's thinking with his own political and religious ideas, and bin Laden provided money and weapons for Zawahiri's Islamic *Jihad*. Zawahiri returned to Afghanistan with bin Laden in 1996 after the Sudanese regime forced him to leave Sudan as a result of Western pressure to hand over bin Laden for his role in numerous terrorist attacks. It was in Afghanistan that the organization known today as *Al Qaeda* really emerged, with Zawahiri as its ideological leader and bin Laden as its "charismatic chieftain."[105]

The Egyptians and their *Salafist* ideology have long been a leading source of global terrorism. Egyptians, including Zawahiri, have exerted great influence on *Al Qaeda*, and continue to hold key positions in the movement. The Egyptian Mohammed Atef was the field commander of *Al Qaeda* until he was killed in Kabul in November 2001. After Atef's death, Sayf al-'Adl, a former colonel in the Egyptian army special forces and head of *Al Qaeda's* media committee, took over as the group's security chief.[106] It seems bin Laden is more of an iconic figurehead at this point, and maybe has been all along. Many observers say Zawahiri manipulated the shy and soft-spoken bin Laden, and according to Burke, "...the sheer number of

---

[104]Ibid, 19.

[105]Ibid, 58.

[106]David Bukay, *From Muhammad to Bin Laden: Religious and Ideological Sources of the Homicide Bombers Phenomenon* (New Brunswick, New Jersey: Transaction Publishers, 2008), 236.

Egyptian militants, all of whom had practical experience of Islamic activism that far outweighed bin Laden's own, raises significant questions about who exactly was in charge of whom."[107]

Full Circle: The Modern-day *Salafi Jihadist* Seeking to Restore the Caliphate – Osama bin Laden (1957 -   ) and *Al Qaeda*

Before looking at bin Laden's background it would be useful to trace the sources of his ideology and review the major themes that formed the basis for his goals. The ideological movement originated with the *Ikhwan* in Saudi Arabia. When the Saudi rulers expelled the *Ikhwan*, the movement migrated to Egypt and influenced the formation of the Muslim Brotherhood. Azzam was a Muslim Brother who studied for his doctorate in Egypt and then went to Saudi Arabia to teach. In the 1960s many of the revolutionary Egyptian Muslim Brothers fled to Saudi Arabia to avoid government prosecution. In Saudi Arabia Azzam met bin Laden and became his teacher and mentor. Azzam and bin Laden went to Pakistan during the Soviet-Afghan War and met Egyptian Brotherhood member Zawahiri, whose influence on bin Laden grew after Azzam's death. Bin Laden returned to Saudi Arabia after the war, until his criticism of the royal family caused the Saudi rulers to expel him and revoke his citizenship. Ultimately bin Laden returned to Afghanistan and announced his *jihad* on America. Bin Laden and Zawahiri envision someday returning to Saudi Arabia and Egypt to overthrow the apostate rulers, truly bringing the movement full circle.

As this Islamic movement evolved, a common set of themes emerged and were advanced by those theologians who most influenced bin Laden. First they all perceived a decline in Islamic society, a society corrupted by apostate rulers and/or external/Western influence. They all sought to attain a more pure and authentic Islamic society ruled by *shari'a*. They believed the only way to achieve this ideal was through *jihad*, and they all agreed that *jihad* was the individual

---

[107]Jason Burke, *Al-Qaeda: The True Story of Radical Islam* (London: I.B. Tauris & Co Ltd, 2006), 150.

obligation of every Muslim. These ideas about what it means to be a true Muslim form the basis of bin Laden's ideology and may lead one to conclude that bin Laden sees himself as a sort of Islamic savior fighting to liberate Muslim lands and restore Islamic authenticity to the *ummah*.

Osama bin Laden's background is almost common knowledge now, as it has been repeatedly recounted in the media since the September 11, 2001 attacks. He was raised the son of a Yemeni construction worker who moved to Saudi Arabia and made a fortune working for the Saudi royal family. He practiced the pure Wahhabi tradition of Islam during his upbringing in Saudi Arabia and, like his mentors, was influenced by the ideas of Ibn Taymiyya and Qutb. Bin Laden attended King Abdul Aziz University in Saudi Arabia, where he was a student of both Azzam and Sayyid Qutb's younger brother Mohammed. According to *The Search for Al Qaeda* author Bruce Riedel, "Azzam introduced Osama to the Palestinian narrative and influenced his view of the conflict with Israel profoundly."[108]

The year 1979 transformed bin Laden's thinking, with several major events that shook the Middle East – the peace treaty between Israel and Egypt; the siege of Mecca; the Iranian Revolution – which demonstrated the possibilities for a successful Islamic movement; and the Soviet invasion of Afghanistan – which served as a rallying force for *jihad*.[109] Though not all sources agree, it is likely Azzam recruited bin Laden into the Muslim Brotherhood and later into the Soviet-Afghan war. Bin Laden used his wealth to aid the Afghan refugees, and he assisted Azzam in the recruitment and training of *jihadists* while forming his own cadre of fighters. Around 1988 bin Laden started calling his fighters "*Al Qaeda al Askariya,*" which means the

---

[108]Burke, 41.

[109]Bukay, 259.

military base, taking the term from Azzam's writing about a vanguard to serve as the strong

foundation – *al-qaeda al-sulbah* – to bring about the new Muslim world.[110]

Bin Laden was back in his homeland of Saudi Arabia after the 1990 Iraq invasion of

Kuwait. He approached the royal family with a proposal to raise an army to protect the Kingdom

from Iraqi forces that were threatening to invade. Instead the leadership formed an alliance with

the United States and allowed American and other allied forces to use Saudi Arabia as an

operational base. Bin Laden grew increasingly critical of the Saudi leaders for allowing

nonbelievers into the holiest of Muslim lands, reminiscent of the *Ikhwan's* anger with the royal

family 60 years earlier over the Western influence they saw corrupting Saudi Arabia. The Saudi

monarchy forced bin Laden to leave the country, and he travelled around - often with Zawahiri,

spending several years in Sudan and eventually returning to Afghanistan in 1996.[111]

Expelling the United States from Muslim lands became a cornerstone of *Al Qaeda*

ideology. According to *Inside Al Qaeda* author Rohan Gunaratna, bin Laden's Muslim supporters

regard him as the "supreme symbol of resistance to US imperialism."[112] In *Knights Under the*

Prophet's Banner, Zawahiri remarked on the galvanizing effect of US presence to rally support

for the *jihad*.[113] In a piece titled *Tactical Recommendations,* bin Laden said, "The first duty and

the best works you can undertake for God is to aim at the Americans and the Jews everywhere on

earth."[114] Within a few months of his return to Afghanistan, bin Laden issued a letter to the entire

ummah calling for *jihad* against Americans and their allies.[115] He specifically referenced the

---

[110]Bruce Riedel, *The Search for* Al Qaeda*: Its Leadership, Ideology, and Future* (Washington, D.C.: Brookings Institution Press, 2008), 45.

[111]Burke, 160.

[112]Rohan Gunaratna, *Inside Al Qaeda: Global Network of Terror* (New York: Berkley Books, 2003), 71.

[113]Kepel and Milelli, 197.

[114]Ibid, 64.

[115]Riedel, 56.

example set by Ibn Taymiyya in his declaration.[116] He was convinced the only way Muslims would be successful at "repelling the invasion" would be by temporarily setting aside their differences and uniting their efforts. Bin Laden emulates Qutb when he presents the West as not at war with *jihadists* but at war with Islam, and he urges Muslims to answers his calls to defend their religion and way of life.[117]

Gunaratna said, "*Al Qaeda* is a political group driven by an interpretive religious ideology."[118] The capacity of *Al Qaeda* to dynamically evolve and adapt to the changing environment in Afghanistan contributes to the elusive nature of the *Al Qaeda* threat. Zawahiri and bin Laden merged their organizations in June 2001 to form *Qaedat al- Jihad*. The formal organization of the original *Al Qaeda* has changed, but it remains an international threat through the perpetuation of its terrorist ideology.[119]

In May 2007 *Al Qaeda* named Mustafa Ahmed Muhammad Uthman Abu al-Yazid, also known as Shaykh Sa'id, as the operational commander for *Al Qaeda* in Afghanistan.[120] Yazid maintains friendly ties with Taliban leadership and his appointment signals the importance for *Al Qaeda* of reestablishing a Taliban-led government in Afghanistan.[121] Yazid, an Egyptian, took part in the Islamist movement in Egypt and, like Zawahiri, was imprisoned for three years following Sadat's assassination. He became a member of Zawahiri's Egyptian Islamic *Jihad* during that time. He went to Afghanistan in 1988 and was one of the core members of *Al Qaeda*

---

[116]Kepel and Milelli, 48-49. Bin Laden quoted Ibn Taymiyya when he discussed the duty of defending Islamic lands against the American invaders: "There is nothing more imperative, after faith, than to repel the aggressor who corrupts religion and life...."

[117]Habeck, 94-96.

[118]Gunaratna, 76.

[119]Bukay, 243-244.

[120]Michael Scheuer, "Al-Qaeda's New Leader in Afghanistan: A Profile of Abu al-Yazid," *Terrorism Focus*, Volume 4, Issue 21 (July 3, 2007), http://www.jamestown.org (accessed 21 August 2009).

[121]Ibid.

at its inception. He took on the role of managing *Al Qaeda*'s finances for bin Laden and was responsible for providing the funds for the 9/11 attacks.[122] During a March 2008 video statement in which Yazid urged professionals like doctors and engineers to join the *jihad*, Yazid quoted Ibn Taymiyya extensively, confirming the continued influence of Taymiyya's ideology on modern-day *jihadists*.[123]

The ideology of *Al Qaeda/Qaedat al-Jihad* aims to achieve phased strategic objectives. The first short-range goal is to cleanse Arab-Muslim states – especially Egypt and Saudi Arabia – from secular and corrupt regimes and replace them with Islamic regimes under *shari'a* law. A second short-term goal is to fight external "infidels" threatening Muslim lands – particularly America and Israel – and free Palestine from its Jewish-Zionist hold. During an interview with *Al Jazeera*, bin Laden said, "What I seek is a right for any living being: that our land be liberated from enemies, liberated from the Americans."[124] He went on to say the United States was depriving Muslims of their manhood, intending to strike a chord with Arab men regarding their courage and ability to defend their family and possessions.[125] Yazid reemphasized this strategy during a July 2008 interview with Pakistani journalist Ahmed Rashid as he stressed that *Al Qaeda* would remain at war with the United States, in part because of American backing of Israel's occupation of Palestine, and that *Al Qaeda* "...would make no distinction between the United States government and ordinary Americans – both would be attacked and killed...."[126] The final short-range goal is to liberate all other Arab Muslim countries. The group's mid-range

[122]Ibid.

[123]The Jamestown Foundation, "Al-Qaeda in Afghanistan Urges Professionals to Joint Mujahideen," *Terrorism Focus*, Volume 5, Issue 11 (March 18, 2008), http://www.jamestown.org (accessed December 10, 2009).

[124]Kepel and Milelli, 58.

[125]Ibid, 59, 285.

[126]Michael Scheuer, "Al-Qaeda's Military Chief in Afghanistan Views the Ongoing Insurgency with Optimism," *Terrorism Focus*, Volume 5, Issue 28 (July 29, 2008), http://www.jamestown.org (accessed December 10, 2009).

goals are to unite all Arab-Muslim lands by reestablishing the *ummah* and to bring back all historic lands conquered by the Muslim dynasties. Both bin Laden and Azzam have pressured Muslims to support this cause by expressing the idea that all Muslims are sinners as long as any country that was once Muslim – for example al-Andalus in Southern Spain – remains under non-Muslim control, and that only those who fight will be absolved from sin.[127] The long-range strategic aim is to bring about "Allah's supreme reign" by bringing the whole world under Islamic law.[128] Bin Laden said, " Our goal, therefore, is to free the land from unbelief, and to apply the law of God there."[129] Ultimately it is this *jihadist* organization that poses the most serious short-term and long-term threat to the United States and its allies and interests because of its stated goals to fight America continuously until the world is united under Islamic law.

Bin Laden formed relationships with local Islamists in Afghanistan, which has likely helped him to evade capture for so many years. Bin Laden, Zawahiri, and *Al Qaeda* aligned with the Taliban, swearing allegiance to its leader, Mullah Omar, and formed a mutually dependent relationship: The Taliban provided *Al Qaeda* protection and hiding, and bin Laden provided funds and fighters for the Taliban. Pakistan initially introduced bin Laden and Omar and encouraged a relationship between them, but the relationship has been tenuous. The Taliban blame bin Laden for the Western presence in the region and the West's interference in Afghanistan in reaction to the 9/11 attacks.[130] Analysts have mixed opinions on the current state of *Al Qaeda*-Taliban relations. Some say there is room to drive a wedge between the groups, while others say the two organizations are now tighter than ever.[131] Internal Taliban

---

[127]Kepel and Milelli, 107, 117.

[128]Bukay, 246-247.

[129]Kepel and Milelli, 59.

[130]Rashid, 139.

[131]Gareth Porter, "Hawks Still Link Taliban to al-Qaeda," *Asia Times* online (October 15, 2009), http://www.atimes.com/atimes/South_Asia/KJ15Df01.html (accessed April 9, 2010).

disagreements have created factions as some Taliban officials indicate they may be willing to negotiate with Afghan President Hamid Karzai, against the desires of Taliban leadership. This division could provide an opportunity for Afghan officials to seek agreements from the Taliban to turn over bin Laden and/or *Al Qaeda* members currently protected by the Taliban.

Pakistan's Role as Protector of the *Jihad*

Pakistan's role goes deeper than just bringing together *Al Qaeda* and the Taliban. During the Soviet-Afghan War the United States covertly supported Afghanistan's Soviet opposition with money and weapons funneled through Pakistan's ISI. Pakistan believed it necessary to intervene in Afghanistan in order to avoid having unfriendly neighbors on both borders and to prevent rival India from extending greater influence among the Afghan factions battling for control.[132] The ISI trained the *mujahidin* fighters and coordinated operations in Afghanistan.[133] After the Soviet withdrawal, the United States turned its back on Pakistan. Pakistan offered support to the Taliban, which they saw as a proxy means for the ISI to maintain control in Afghanistan. The Taliban and bin Laden provided training for Pakistan-based Kashmiri militants, so Pakistan has not been inclined to help the United States conduct operations to kill or capture bin Laden.[134] Overt Pakistani support to the Taliban ended after the 9/11 attacks when the government agreed to side with the United States, but Pakistan remains torn between its assurances to the West and its Islamic ties to the region. As recently as 2008 Pakistan cut peace deals with *Al Qaeda* and the Taliban, enabling the jihadists to regroup before renewing attacks on Pakistani forces.[135]

---

[132]Rohan Gunaratna, *Inside Al Qaeda: Global Network of Terror* (New York: Berkley Books, 2003), 53.

[133]Riedel, 62.

[134]Rashid, 137-178.

[135]Moorthy S. Muthuswamy, *Defeating Political Islam: The New Cold War* (Amherst, NY: Prometheus Books, 2009), 183.

Meanwhile Pakistan continues to receive financial aid from the United States as long as the *jihadist* threat remains.

The Taliban, with help from Pakistan and *Al Qaeda,* achieved its goal in Afghanistan for a limited time, and continues to fight for the opportunity to do so again. While it had been in Pakistan's best interest to support installation of a government that would be favorable to Pakistan – as an ally against Iran and India – Pakistan's own government is now at risk and cannot control the *jihadist* activity in the border region it shares with Afghanistan.[136] *Al Qaeda* operatives have tried in the past to procure some type of weapon of mass destruction (WMD) and bin Laden has indicated his desire as well as the Islamic legitimacy to use such a device against the United States or Israel as part of the defensive *jihad.*[137] Bin Laden said of acquiring nuclear weapons:

> To seek to possess the weapons that could counter those of the infidels is a religious duty. If I have indeed acquired these weapons, then this is an obligation I carried out.... And if I seek to acquire these weapons I am carrying out a duty. It would be a sin for Muslims not to try to possess the weapons that would prevent the infidels from inflicting harm on Muslims.[138]

Pakistan is the most likely source for Al Qaeda's acquisition of a nuclear weapon. According to author Bruce Riedel, "The greatest possible threat is that al Qaeda will recruit a senior Pakistani

---

[136]"With the current situation in Afghanistan – the U.S. and NATO failing to control the country, while it slips back into the same kind of anarchy as after the Soviet invasion – Pakistan retains the most vital interest in its stability, under a compatible regime, preferably one it can control." Stephen Tanner, *Afghanistan: A Military History from Alexander the Great to the War Against the Taliban,* updated version (Philadelphia: Da Capo Press, 2009), 324-325, 336, 346-348.

[137]"Bin Laden is not interested in using a CBRN weapon to terrorize his foes; he is seeking a first-strike capability, a strategic not a tactical weapon." Gunaratna, 66; Michael Scheuer, *Through Our Enemies' Eyes: Osama Bin Laden, Radical Islam, and the Future of America* (Washington, DC: Brassey's Inc., 2003), 68. In September 1999 bin Laden supporter Omar Bakri Muhammed wrote a letter telling bin Laden use of biological weapons in self-defense is permissible in Islam. Bakri said he believed bin Laden's *jihad* was defensive, a point bin Laden himself continues to emphasize in his speeches.

[138]Gunaratna, 65.

military officer in control of some part of the national arsenal, who may then secretly pass one or two weapons to the terrorists....″[139]

Al Qaeda considers Pakistan its global operations base. Bin Laden wants Afghanistan and Pakistan to form the core of a new caliphate in South Asia.[140] Pakistan is central to bin Laden's vision for a future Islamic world, and it would seem many Pakistanis favor the jihadis over the United States as stabilizers in the region. A May-June 2008 poll showed the Pakistani population favored negotiating with Al Qaeda and the Taliban over fighting them, fifty-two percent hold the United States responsible for violence in Pakistan, and seventy-nine percent agreed with imposing a strict application of shari'a in Islamic countries.[141] In a July 2009 Gallup Pakistan poll, forty-three percent of those surveyed believed the Pakistani government should have a dialogue with the Taliban, and believed the United States posed the greatest threat to Pakistan, more so than both the Taliban and India.[142]

How to Fight an Ideology

> The center of the jihadist movement is its ideology, which must be directly confronted, challenged, and defeated.
>
> - Mary Habeck, Knowing the Enemy

The previous sections present the major Islamic concepts behind bin Laden's jihadist ideology. Bin Laden has been able to present his cause as the fulfillment of a Muslim obligation and a way to create a more authentic Islamic society for all Muslims. Understanding that the United States must overcome this ideology rather than a particular person or organization is key to driving formation of proper responses to the Al Qaeda threat. Al Qaeda does not have to

---

[139]Riedel, 133.

[140]Ibid, 125; Lawrence, 30.

[141]Muthuswamy, 184.

[142]Al Jazeera-Gallup Pakistan Survey, "Pakistan: State of the Nation," August 13, 2009, Aljazeera.net, http://english.aljazeera.net/ focus/2009/08/2009888238994769.html#threat (accessed August 12, 2009).

decisively defeat the United States military in order to achieve success – it just has to survive in order to discredit American might and outlast American will. *Jihadists* think about stages of Islamic conquest over the long term – they are not constrained by 4-year election cycles or year-long deployment rotations. American strategy must also focus on a long-term solution in order to devise an acceptable and achievable end state.

While *Al Qaeda* has no established set of rules or an explicit plan of action, it promotes employment of certain methods which include terror and violence against Arab-Islamic regimes; delegitimizing corrupt Islamic regimes; conducting terror attacks against Western nations in order to cause these nations to withdraw military and civilian personnel from Muslim lands; and portraying the United States and Israel as evil "Satans" – the real underlying causes for *Al Qaeda* terror and violence and the reason for world instability and lack of peace.[143] Bin Laden portrays the *jihad* as defensive, a reaction to the Western threat to Islam's existence. By making the West, and especially the United States, responsible for the world's problems, *Al Qaeda* hopes to isolate the United States from potential external allies as well as to turn public support against the American government.[144]

Jihadists Continue the Struggle –The Current Environment of Afghanistan

Bin Laden has managed to avoid capture and *Al Qaeda* has avoided decisive defeat, so it remains a threat to United States and NATO forces as it continues toward achievement of its strategic objectives. *Al Qaeda* operations in Afghanistan are heaviest in the Afghan provinces bordering Pakistan's Federally Administered Tribal Area (FATA), *Al Qaeda's* current operational base. Attacks consist mainly of Improvised Explosive Devices and rocket and mortar attacks, but *Al Qaeda* fighters also participate in Taliban ground attacks against Afghan security forces or

---

[143]Bukay, 247.

[144]Michael Scheuer, *Through Our Enemies' Eyes: Osama Bin Laden, Radical Islam, and the Future of America*, 228-229; Bukay, 273.

NATO troops, and *Al Qaeda* has carried out several suicide attacks in Afghanistan.[145]

United States and NATO casualties in Afghanistan reached an all-time high at the end of 2008, while the Taliban and its allies either controlled or had destabilized more than two-thirds of the country.[146] United States allies are convinced the war in Afghanistan cannot be won, but could be brought to a level manageable by the Afghan Army.[147] The Afghan government of Hamid Karzai cannot afford to maintain its NATO-built Army.[148] Neither Afghanistan nor Pakistan can control the tribal areas of Pashtunistan.[149] Pakistani officials have urged NATO countries to accept the Taliban.[150] Looking for a way to achieve peace, or at least a more permanent stability, Karzai opened talks with the Taliban in 2008.[151] Sometime in early 2010 Karzai plans to offer Taliban militants jobs and a guarantee that they would not be arrested by Afghan or international security forces in exchange for their agreement to stop fighting.[152] According to a February 2010 *Newsweek* article, Karzai's plan will not work:

---

[145]"The authors believe that aside from *Al Qaeda's* support for the Taliban's fight in Afghanistan, their involvement in IED, mortar, and rocket attacks is primarily intended to create footage for propaganda purposes and train their cadre before they are sent back to their respective countries." Rohan Gunaratna and Anders Nielsen, "*Al Qaeda* in the Tribal Areas Between Afghanistan and Pakistan," *Studies in Conflict & Terrorism* 31 (2008):786.

[146]Stephen Tanner, *Afghanistan: A Military History from Alexander the Great to the War Against the Taliban* (Updated version, Philadelphia: Da Capo Press, 2009), 344.

[147]Ibid, 344.

[148]Ibid.

[149]Ibid, 325. Pashtunistan straddles the Afghanistan-Pakistan border, invalidating the traditional border which had originally been drawn in 1893 to split the Pashtun, who are the world's largest remaining tribal-based society. Pashtunistan lies more in Pakistan than Afghanistan and includes the Northwest Frontier Province and Federally Administered Tribal Area in Pakistan, as well as major cities in Afghanistan including Kandahar and Kabul.

[150]Muthuswamy, 27.

[151]"Karzai was pursuing the age-old imperative of Afghan rulers to forge alliances internally, finally realizing full well that the country could not permanently be subdued by force alone." Tanner, 343, 345-347.

[152]Damien McElroy, "Afghan *Loya Jirga* to promote Taliban reconciliation," Telegraph.co.uk (January 28, 2010), http://www.telegraph.co.uk/news/worldnews/asia/afghanistan/7093344/Afghan-Loya-Jirga-to-promote-Taliban-reconciliation.html (accessed March 21, 2010).

> [The Taliban] insist they have a sacred duty to drive the invaders out of
> Afghanistan, return Mullah Omar's self-proclaimed Islamic Emirate to power,
> and reimpose his merciless version of Islamic law throughout the land. "In the
> next few months we will prove this is not a fight for power, for land, or for
> becoming president, but for Islam, ideology, and *jihad*," says a top Taliban
> official....[153]

The United States has not defeated the Taliban – the *jihadis* deserted the cities in order to survive. In reality the United States may have done the group a favor by removing them from power, because the former governing organization no longer has the burden of caring for the population. The Taliban has resorted to its original state of insurgency – it does not hold or have to defend territory in Afghanistan and has time on its side to wait out United States resolve. Karzai's government rules Kabul and its immediate surroundings while still being propped up by the United States, and beyond Kabul the warlords have reemerged. The population believes the country experienced less internal fighting when the Taliban was in control.[154]

The Afghan people suffer as they are caught in the middle of the turmoil just trying to survive. The continuing civil war has created the largest refugee population in the world.[155] According to *Taliban* author Ahmed Rashid, "A mixture of fear, acceptance, total exhaustion and devastation after years of war... forced many Afghans to accept the Taliban ways of justice."[156] The Taliban has conducted talks with Karzai's government, and the group's desire for survival and recognition as a legitimate government could cause them to negotiate some of their extreme terms, like those involving human rights, to make a Taliban-led government more acceptable to

---

[153]Ron Moreau and Sami Yousafzai, "Turning the Taliban," Newsweek.com (February 12, 2010), http://www.newsweek.com/id/233590?obref=obnetwork (accessed March 25, 2010).

[154]Michael Scheuer, *Through Our Enemies' Eyes: Osama Bin Laden, Radical Islam, and the Future of America*, 249-250.

[155]Rashid, xiii.

[156]Ibid, 4.

the West and other Muslim nations.[157] After all this time the people likely just want to see an end

to the fighting and achieve a real sense of security and stability - no matter who provides it.[158]

How Should the United States Respond? Recommendations for Defeating the *Jihadist* Narrative

> If you want to make friends with Arabs, you have to be sensitive to how they view things.
> - Yitzhak Rabin, *Talking to Terrorists*

> We are only now beginning to realize that the reason we have failed to communicate our message is that we don't have one.
> - Mark Perry, *Talking to Terrorists*

The Islamic *jihad* is a war of attrition with a timeline that spans decades. *Al Qaeda*

poses a constantly changing and evolving threat. United States strategic policy must change and

evolve as well in order to effectively counter this threat. In order to do that, the United States

must develop a better understanding of the *jihadist* ideology and the concepts that drive support

for bin Laden and *Al Qaeda*. Bin Laden's *jihadist* narrative is deeply rooted in Islamic history

and tradition, and understanding the development of his ideology is crucial for understanding the

current strategic problem. Strategic thinking and planning must reach beyond the current

generation of *jihadists* and consider ways to influence the next generation as well, addressing the

root causes of conflict instead of continuing to battle against the symptoms.[159] Strategy must

include real measures of effectiveness. The standard kill-capture metric has no relevance or

context when the total number of opposition fighters is unknown, when killing one *jihadist* results

in several new *jihadi* recruits seeking to avenge the death of their friend or family member, or

when the enemy believes he is fighting for God's will and dying as a martyr. *Al Qaeda* has no

---

[157]M.J. Gohari, *The Taliban: Ascent to Power* (London: Oxford University Press, 2001), 149.

[158]Carol Graham and Jenny Shapiro, "Why Are Afghans Smiling?," *Washington Post*, August 13, 2009, http://www.washingtonpost.com/wp-dyn/content/article/2009/08/10/AR2009081002456.html (accessed August 13, 2009).

[159]Bruce Hoffman, "Al Qaeda Then and Now," in *Al Qaeda Now: Understanding Today's Terrorists*, ed. Karen J. Greenberg (New York, NY: Cambridge University Press, 2005), 11.

intention of ending the *jihad* – lest one forget Azzam's central theme of the unending and eternal *jihad*. If America no longer "occupies" Muslim lands, *Al Qaeda* has only achieved its near-term objective. Bin Laden's ultimate desire is to restore the caliphate and to bring the whole world under Islamic law.

The threat posed by bin Laden is more than just a military one. Through the continued use of propaganda to promote its goals and tarnish United States and Western involvement in the region, *Al Qaeda* threatens Americans in Afghanistan and around the world. *Inside Al Qaeda* author Gunaratna warned, "In the absence of a powerfully articulated counterideology, *Al Qaeda* can come to represent the truth for some Muslims."[160] American leadership must take bin Laden's speeches seriously and not simply dismiss his messages as crazy banter and meaningless rhetoric. Thousands of young men joined the *jihad* because *they* believed in bin Laden's message and were willing to die and become martyrs in the defense of Islam and to achieve an ideal Islamic society.[161] Not all Islamists condone bin Laden's actions, but they also do not condemn bin Laden because he fights for the cause of Islam and gave up his fortune and future prospects to wage *jihad*.[162]

Developing new messages to counter *Al Qaeda's* Islamic narrative is vital. The United States must find ways to challenge and discredit the Islamic-ness of bin Laden's ideology and *Al Qaeda's* actions in order to reduce the opposition's base of support.[163] The United States should maximize its use of Arabic-speaking Americans and Arabic media outlets to ensure its message reaches the intended Muslim audience. Even better would be to form a Western-Arab information partnership, so Muslims take the lead in creating messages to counter bin Laden's

---

[160]Rohan Gunaratna, *Inside Al Qaeda: Global Network of Terror* (New York: Berkley Books, 2003), 19.

[161]Lawrence, 24-30.

[162]Michael Scheuer, *Through Our Enemies' Eyes: Osama Bin Laden, Radical Islam, and the Future of America,* 257.

[163]Ibid, 315.

jihadist ideology. At the same time America must work to create an environment of tolerance and change Muslim perceptions about modernity and the West that *Al Qaeda* uses to garner support. Hostility toward America is not limited to *jihadists* – many Muslims have anti-American feelings, as evidenced in the polls of the Pakistani population referenced earlier in this paper. According to Jeff Aronson, director of research and publications at the Foundation for Middle East Peace, "We have to come to terms with a disturbing and blunt truth... that after 9/11 a segment of our planet celebrated. We cannot simply pass it off; we cannot ignore it."[164] Mark Perry, author of *Talking to Terrorists*, continued Aronson's thought: "We cannot simply condemn that celebration as the work of people who 'do not share our values.' We must find out why they celebrated."[165]

As part of this campaign to win Muslim support, the United States must make a concerted effort to pull potential *jihadi* recruits away from the lure of *Al Qaeda*. The attraction of bin Laden's ideology combined with the more obvious issues of un-democratic governments, poverty, and poor education, create a complex situation that enhances bin Laden's narrative. The Middle East suffers from a huge youth bulge that has led to a group of poor, unhappy, and unemployed young men. Many of these youth turn to the free education offered in Deobandi and Taliban *madrassas* that support the *jihad* and point to the West being responsible for the existing social conditions. With no other options for their future, many of these young men join the *jihad*. Financial aid to expand education opportunities and employment programs aimed at improving local infrastructure would help stem the tide of *jihadi* recruits. State-funded and administered programs that provide a more unbiased and less militant religious education and vocational training may rebuild confidence in local governments and reduce the recruiting pool for *Al*

---

[164]Mark Perry, *Talking to Terrorists: Why America Must Engage with its Enemies* (New York: Basic Books, 2010), 213.

[165]Ibid.

Qaeda. To be effective the current system must ultimately transform to produce a more desired end state – for both the Arab world and the West – of a secure, politically stable, and economically sufficient environment.

Globalization and Westernization have shown the already poor and oppressed more things they cannot have while creating a sense of fear among Muslim fundamentalists who reject Western innovation.[166] Many Muslims have the perception that the United States controls everything, so why has the United States not fixed the problems of the Middle East? *Islamic Extremism* authors Monte and Princess Palmer explain:

> Perhaps the most widely held of all Middle Eastern perceptions of the United States is the belief that little of importance happens in the region, if not the world, that is not the direct result of American manipulation...If the United States really controls everything, why is the region slipping under the control of extremists? Why hasn't the Arab-Israeli crisis been resolved?... Why does bin Laden's *al Qaeda* network remain at large?[167]

Unstable or unpopular governments add to this perception by shifting blame for regional problems on the United States and Western imperialism to avoid taking responsibility for their own social and economic problems, thus creating intense feelings of bitterness and hatred toward the American government.[168] Bin Laden contributes to this anti-American sentiment by calling out United States faults – America is the aggressor, is un-Islamic, and is a supporter of Israel .[169] The US-based Arabic satellite television network, *Al-Hurra*, has not achieved great success with

---

[166]"Many are lured by the promise of westernization. The devout have recoiled in fear that traditional Islamic values are being irrevocably destroyed. Both sides are fearful and frustrated, the former by what they can't have and the latter by what they might lose." Monte Palmer and Princess Palmer, *Islamic Extremism: Causes, Diversity, and Challenges* (Lanham, MD: Rowman & Littlefield Publishers, 2008), 18.

[167]Palmer and Palmer, 29.

[168]Ibid, 30.

[169]Lawrence, 161-175. In his letter to the Americans dated October 6, 2002, which was posted to the internet in Arabic on October 14, 2002, bin Laden said, "It is saddening to tell you that you are the worst civilization witnessed in the history of mankind." See APPENDIX C for more excerpts from the letter.

Middle Eastern viewers who find the programming boring.[170] The channel may be more successful in appealing to Arab viewers if the United States uses the channel to launch propaganda discrediting political Islam and the *jihad*. These types of programs would be controversial and may draw viewers away from Arab-based media, like *Al-Jazeera*.[171]

In order to overcome Muslim perceptions of ineffectiveness, the United States must focus more effort on finding bin Laden. It is not likely that bin Laden would allow himself to be taken alive, rather he would choose to die fighting and become a martyr for his cause. During a March 1997 interview with CNN reporter Peter Arnett, bin Laden said:

> We see that getting killed in the cause of God is a great honor wished for by our Prophet. He said in his *hadith*: 'I swear to God, I wish to fight for God's cause and be killed, I'll do it again....' Being killed for God's cause is a great honor achieved by only those who are the elite of the nation. We love this kind of death for God's cause as much as you like to live... It's something we wish for.[172]

Bin Laden's death and martyrdom could have the immediate effect of retaliatory attacks against America and the West. Killing bin Laden would initially weaken *Al Qaeda* and the *jihad*. In the long term bin Laden's death would draw even more attention to his actions and messages, thereby raising support for *Al Qaeda* and the global *jihad*, so ultimately it would be better to capture bin Laden alive than to kill him.[173] America's top commander in Afghanistan, General Stanley McChrystal, told reporters on March 17, 2010, that the United States is still committed to capturing bin Laden alive. Capturing bin Laden would most likely lead to deadly mass terrorist reprisals or kidnapping of key United States officials in an attempt to trade for bin Laden's release. However subjecting bin Laden to the same type of post-capture examinations and media

---

[170]Muthuswamy, 171-172.

[171]Ibid.

[172]Lawrence, 56.

[173]Peter Bergen, "*Al Qaeda* Then and Now," In *Al Qaeda Now: Understanding Today's Terrorists*, ed. Karen J. Greenberg (New York: Cambridge University Press, 2005), 4.

displays as Saddam Hussein experienced could actually deflate bin Laden's mythical character and diminish support to his cause.[174]

The United States has to understand not only *Al Qaeda's* ideology, but also gain a firm understanding about the environment and culture of Afghanistan. Afghanistan is traditionally a tribal-based society. According to United States strategic analyst Ralph Peters, by backing a central government in Kabul the United States is "...imagining a state that has never existed in Afghanistan."[175] The state has always been the enemy of tribal warlords, so the Taliban gained popularity as a government opposition movement, even if the system they imposed seemed brutal and intolerant.[176] If tribalism has more meaning to the Afghan people than nationalism, then building up the tribes may have more long-term value for defeating *Al Qaeda*. Bin Laden, Zawahiri and their "Arab Afghans" are outsiders whose actions initiated the American response and its continued presence in Afghanistan. Strengthening the tribal base and creating a wedge between Afghans and *Al Qaeda* enables the population to deal with its own problem. The Pashtun tribe still holds the majority and tribal rivalries will almost certainly arise, but that has been the natural order of Afghanistan for centuries. According to United States Army Special Forces Major Jim Gant, "The only existing structure that offers governance and security for the Afghan people is at the tribal level. We should leverage this and use it to our advantage—before it is too late."[177]

While developing a whole-of-government approach to Afghanistan is vital, one cannot overlook the fact that a military problem still exists in Afghanistan. Since his April 1996 Declaration of *Jihad* against America, Bin Laden has made clear his objective to drive the United

---

[174]Ibid.

[175]Ralph Peters (lecture, Command and General Staff College, Fort Leavenworth, KS, March 10, 2010).

[176] Ibid.

[177]Jim Gant, Major, US Army Special Forces, *One Tribe at a Time: A Strategy for Success in Afghanistan*, 2nd ed. (Los Angeles: Nine Sisters Imports Inc, 2009), 13.

States out of Muslim lands, "...to expel them in defeat and humiliation from the holy places of Islam."[178]

During a March 10, 2010, lecture at the Command and General Staff College in Fort Leavenworth, Kansas, Ralph Peters said that *Al Qaeda*, not the Taliban, is the real threat to the United States, and that diplomacy will not change the beliefs of religious insurgents – the only way to stop them is with bullets. According to Peters, "You don't break the enemy's will with aid programs."[179] The first step for the United States is to prevent the *jihadists* from killing more people, and that means United States and coalition military forces have to kill them first. The United States must not focus its resources and efforts on all extremists at once, but instead place priority on those who pose the biggest threat to America's security – and right now that is *Al Qaeda*.

If bin Laden is killed or the leadership structure begins to suffer from increased military operations and pressure, the core organization will most likely relocate to a more permissive environment, like it did when moving to Sudan in the 1990s. In *Knight's Under the Prophet's Banner* Zawahiri acknowledges the necessity of moving the group's leaders and key members to safety if the movement's existence is threatened.[180] Because of Zawahiri's influence, the less than stable regime, and the fact that Egyptians comprise the largest group of *Al Qaeda* members, Egypt is one location for a new *Al Qaeda* base. More likely, especially if bin Laden is alive, is Yemen. Bin Laden's father was from Yemen, bin Laden's fourth wife is Yemeni, Yemenis make up the third largest segment of *Al Qaeda* members, and bin Laden has previously considered Yemen as an alternate base location.[181] The Muslim Brotherhood, which shares *Al Qaeda's*

---

[178]Lawrence, 30.

[179]Ralph Peters (lecture, Command and General Staff College, Fort Leavenworth, KS, March 10, 2010).

[180]Lawrence, 200.

[181]Gunaratna, 186.

ideology, is a prevalent political organization in Yemen.[182] Yemen borders Saudi Arabia and though his Saudi citizenship was revoked, bin Laden still receives funding through charitable donations from supportive Saudi citizens.[183] Yemen's terrain is heavily mountainous, providing opportunities for seclusion and shelter, and Yemen's tribal-based culture is majority Sunni – similar to *Al Qaeda's* current conditions in the tribal border regions of Afghanistan and Pakistan.[184] The Yemeni government has been unable to control and influence the majority of its territory and has been weakened by internal separatist fighting as well as a pre-existing *Al Qaeda* insurgency that could set the conditions for the group relocating from Afghanistan.[185] The United States should take steps now to make conditions "inhospitable" in potential future base locations and give *Al Qaeda* nowhere to run.

Conclusion

Bin Laden has clearly stated his goals supported by a historical narrative about true and authentic Islam, and he has laid out the strategy *Al Qaeda* will implement to attain its desired end state. Developing an understanding of the *jihadist* ideology is the only way America can build an effective strategy to counter bin Laden and *Al Qaeda*. It requires more than bullets to fight an ideology. According to Bard O'Neill, whose book *Insurgency and Terrorism* provides a framework for analyzing insurgencies, "A government that misunderstands the type of insurgent movement it is facing can blind itself to policy options... Conversely, one that does understand is in a better position to craft appropriate and rational responses."[186] This concept of learning about

---

[182]Palmer and Palmer, 48.

[183]Michael Scheuer, *Through Our Enemies' Eyes: Osama Bin Laden, Radical Islam, and the Future of America*, 37-39; Muthuswamy, 195.

[184]Lawrence, 41. In a November 1996 interview with Bari Atwan, editor of London-based newspaper *Al-Quds Al-Arabi*, bin Laden contemplated leaving Afghanistan for Yemen "...with its armed tribesmen, mountainous terrain, and clear air you can breathe without humiliation."

[185]Gunaratna, 186.

[186]Bard E. O'Neill, *Insurgency & Terrorism: From Revolution to Apocalypse,* 2nd ed. (Washington, DC: Potomac Books, Inc., 2005), 157.

the true nature of opposition in order to form appropriate responses applies not just to the *Al Qaeda* threat, but to any form of opposition the United States faces. For the purpose of this monograph, the focus is *Al Qaeda* in Afghanistan and Pakistan.

The people of Afghanistan have defied conquest for more than 2,500 years. Afghanistan today is returning to a state of tribal anarchy. The Taliban and *Al Qaeda* have made a resurgence in the Pashtun region and across the border in Pakistan.[187] No central authority has had lasting success in Afghanistan – eventually authority always reverts back to the control of tribal leaders. The United States must prepare to accept that outcome in Afghanistan if Karzai's government collapses.[188]   Ultimately the *jihadist* movement arose out of a question of *identity*. What does it mean to be a Muslim? What is true and authentic Islam? The Islamic identity transcends any sense of nationalism. If Islam is in a state of decline, who is to blame? "Us" or "Them"? Bin Laden has cast America as the aggressor, a single target to unify a defensive *jihadist* campaign. American leadership must understand this concept, because it is how *Al Qaeda* built its following. The *jihadist* war is a struggle over who will control the future of Islam . The prevailing Muslim voice essentially becomes the voice for all of Islam.[189] Unless he is challenged from within Muslim society, that voice is a Zawahiri-influenced Osama bin Laden's, and the message will be *jihad* until his goals are realized.[190]

Bin Laden mastered the application of historical context to make it relevant to the modern-day *jihad*. *Al Qaeda* is rooted in the past, but remains a modern threat through its adaptive nature – forming alliances with other *jihadist* organizations like the Taliban to ensure survival and using technology to spread the message of *jihad* and rally continued support. Bin

---

[187]Tanner, 337.

[188]Gant, 12.

[189]Habeck, 164, 173.

[190]Muthuswamy, 192-194.

Laden's ideology continues to uphold the core concepts of some of the most noted Islamic *Salafist* theologians – from Ibn Taymiyya to al-Wahhab to Sayyid Qutb. These predecessors give legitimacy to *Al Qaeda's* actions – they all looked back to the time of the Prophet as the ideal, the most true and pure Islamic society. This is what bin Laden promotes in order to keep his following – the most faithful Muslims throughout time participated in *jihad* to bring about a return to a pure and authentic Islam; a society governed by *shari'a*, based on the *Qur'an*; a way to restore the Muslim caliphate – and the United States is preventing achievement of that ideal. Zawahiri urges *jihadis* to carry out attacks that inflict maximum casualties because "this is the language understood by the West," and tells *jihadis* to concentrate on martyrdom operations as the most successful way to inflict damage on the United States.[191] As long as bin Laden and Zawahiri are able to continue recruiting devoted Muslims to their calls of *jihad*, *Al Qaeda*'s *jihadist* ideology will remain a threat to America and the West.

There are many competing interests in Afghanistan: America, bin Laden and *Al Qaeda*, the Taliban, the current Afghan government and Afghani population, Pakistan, Saudi Arabia, the NATO alliance, and others. The United States must develop a new understanding about the environment and the problem it faces in Afghanistan – what *Al Qaeda* struggles to achieve, why bin Laden formed the ideology he projects through *Al Qaeda*, why so many Muslims support bin Laden and agree with his message, and why many Muslims have a negative sentiment about America and its involvement in the region. By learning about this complex problem in Afghanistan and Pakistan, American leadership will be more prepared to design an effective strategy and plan operations aimed at achieving an end state that is acceptable to those involved.

---

[191]Gilles Kepel and Jean-Pierre Milelli, ed. Translated by Pascale Ghazaleh. *Al Qaeda in its Own Words* (Cambridge, Mass.: Belknap Press of Harvard University Press, 2008), 203-204.

APPENDIX A – Deobandism

According to Jason Burke in his book *Al-Qaeda: The True Story of Radical Islam*:

It is easy to confuse political Islamism and the strand of Islamic thought derived from the early Deobandis, yet the two are very different. Where political Islamism is focused on the Islamicization of the state through what are effectively political channels, the Deobandis reject politics altogether. The emphasis placed by the Deobandis on a rigid observance of a literal reading of *Qur'anic* injunctions is very different from the relative flexibility of the political Islamists. And where political Islamists... reject the authority of the ulema, the Deobandis venerate the clergy and recognize their monopoly on textual interpretation.[192]

The Deobandis first arose in British India in the mid-1800s as a forward-looking movement to unite Muslims struggling to live in a non-Muslim colonial state. Through education in their many *madrassas* the Deobandis aimed to teach Muslims how to interpret *shari'a* law in terms of current realities. According to Taliban biographer Ahmed Rashid, "The Deobandis took a restrictive view of the role of women, opposed all forms of hierarchy in the Muslim community and rejected the Shia – but the Taliban were to take these beliefs to an extreme...."[193]

---

[192]Jason Burke, *Al-Qaeda: The True Story of Radical Islam* (London: I.B. Tauris & Co Ltd, 2006), 92.

[193]Ahmed Rashid, *Taliban: Militant Islam, Oil and Fundamentalism in Central Asia* (New Haven: Yale University Press, 2001), 88.

APPENDIX B - The Kharijites

The Arabic word *kharaja* means "to go out." The Kharijites were Muslim dissidents who chose to separate themselves from the mainstream of society, believing the majority of Muslims had strayed from the true path of Islam. The Kharijites declared *jihad* against all Muslims who they considered unbelievers and apostates and carried out violence and assassinations, including the killing of Ali, the fourth Caliph and cousin of the Prophet Muhammad in 661. Kharijites believed it took more than a profession of faith for one to be a true Muslim and divided the world into the realm of true Muslims and the realm of nonbelievers. The Kharijites developed a following among non-Arab Muslims who felt oppressed and discriminated against by Arab rulers. Kharijites preached that a return to "a more pure form of Islam" would solve society's economic and social problems.[194]

---

[194] Austin Cline, "Islam and Muslims: Kharijites," About.com: Agnosticism/Atheism, http://atheism.about.com/library/ FAQs/islam/blfaq_islam_kharijites.htm (accessed December 6, 2009).

APPENDIX C – Excerpts from Bin Laden's Letter to the Americans, October 6, 2002[195]

In the Name of Allah, the Most Gracious, the Most Merciful,

> Permission to fight (against disbelievers) is given to those (believers) who are fought against, because they have been wronged and surely, Allah is Able to give them (believers) victory. [Quran 22:39]

> Those who believe, fight in the Cause of Allah, and those who disbelieve, fight in the cause of Taghut (anything worshipped other than Allah e.g. Satan). So fight you against the friends of Satan; ever feeble is indeed the plot of Satan. [Quran 4:76]

Some American writers have published articles under the title 'On what basis are we fighting?' These articles have generated a number of responses, some of which adhered to the truth and were based on Islamic Law, and others which have not. Here we wanted to outline the truth - as an explanation and warning - hoping for Allah's reward, seeking success and support from Him.

While seeking Allah's help, we form our reply based on two questions directed at the Americans:

(Q1) Why are we fighting and opposing you?
(Q2) What are we calling you to, and what do we want from you?

As for the first question: Why are we fighting and opposing you? The answer is very simple:

(1) Because you attacked us and continue to attack us.

a) You attacked us in Palestine:

(i) Palestine, which has sunk under military occupation for more than 80 years. The British handed over Palestine, with your help and your support, to the Jews, who have occupied it for more than 50 years; years overflowing with oppression, tyranny, crimes, killing, expulsion, destruction and devastation. The creation and continuation of Israel is one of the greatest crimes, and you are the leaders of its criminals. And of course there is no need to explain and prove the degree of American support for Israel. The creation of Israel is a crime which must be erased. Each and every person whose hands have become polluted in the contribution towards this crime must pay its price, and pay for it heavily.

. . .

(b) You attacked us in Somalia; you supported the Russian atrocities against us in Chechnya, the Indian oppression against us in Kashmir, and the Jewish aggression against us in Lebanon.

---

[195]Bruce Lawrence, ed., *Messages to the World: The Statements of Osama Bin Laden*, trans. James Howarth (London: Verso, 2005), 161-175.

(c) Under your supervision, consent and orders, the governments of our countries which act as your agents, attack us on a daily basis;

(i) These governments prevent our people from establishing the Islamic Shariah, using violence and lies to do so.

. . .

(iii) These governments steal our Ummah's wealth and sell them to you at a paltry price.

. . .

(v) The removal of these governments is an obligation upon us, and a necessary step to free the Ummah, to make the Shariah the supreme law and to regain Palestine. And our fight against these governments is not separate from out fight against you.

(d) You steal our wealth and oil at paltry prices because of you international influence and military threats. This theft is indeed the biggest theft ever witnessed by mankind in the history of the world.

(e) Your forces occupy our countries; you spread your military bases throughout them; you corrupt our lands, and you besiege our sanctities, to protect the security of the Jews and to ensure the continuity of your pillage of our treasures.

. . .

(2) These tragedies and calamities are only a few examples of your oppression and aggression against us. It is commanded by our religion and intellect that the oppressed have a right to return the aggression. Do not await anything from us but Jihad, resistance and revenge. Is it in any way rational to expect that after America has attacked us for more than half a century, that we will then leave her to live in security and peace?!!

. . .

(f) Allah, the Almighty, legislated the permission and the option to take revenge. Thus, if we are attacked, then we have the right to attack back. Whoever has destroyed our villages and towns, then we have the right to destroy their villages and towns. Whoever has stolen our wealth, then we have the right to destroy their economy. And whoever has killed our civilians, then we have the right to kill theirs.

The American Government and press still refuses to answer the question:

Why did they attack us in New York and Washington?

. . .

(Q2) As for the second question that we want to answer: What are we calling you to, and what do we want from you?

(1) The first thing that we are calling you to is Islam.

(a) The religion of the Unification of God; of freedom from associating partners with Him, and rejection of this; of complete love of Him, the Exalted; of complete submission to His Laws; and of the discarding of all the opinions, orders, theories and religions which contradict with the religion He sent down to His Prophet Muhammad (peace be upon him). Islam is the religion of all the prophets, and makes no distinction between them - peace be upon them all.

. . .

(b) It is saddening to tell you that you are the worst civilization witnessed by the history of mankind:

. . .

(ii) You are the nation that permits Usury, which has been forbidden by all the religions. Yet you build your economy and investments on Usury. As a result of this, in all its different forms and guises, the Jews have taken control of your economy, through which they have then taken control of your media, and now control all aspects of your life making you their servants and achieving their aims at your expense; precisely what Benjamin Franklin warned you against.

. . .

Who can forget your President Clinton's immoral acts committed in the official Oval office? After that you did not even bring him to account, other than that he 'made a mistake', after which everything passed with no punishment. Is there a worse kind of event for which your name will go down in history and remembered by nations?

. . .

(xi) That which you are singled out for in the history of mankind, is that you have used your force to destroy mankind more than any other nation in history; not to defend principles and values, but to hasten to secure your interests and profits. You who dropped a nuclear bomb on Japan, even though Japan was ready to negotiate an end to the war. How many acts of oppression, tyranny and injustice have you carried out, O callers to freedom?

(xii) Let us not forget one of your major characteristics: your duality in both manners and values; your hypocrisy in manners and principles. All manners, principles and values have two scales: one for you and one for the others.

. . .

(b) Your policy on prohibiting and forcibly removing weapons of mass destruction to ensure world peace: it only applies to those countries which you do not permit to possess such weapons. As for the countries you consent to, such as Israel, then they are allowed to keep and use such weapons to defend their security. Anyone else who you suspect might be manufacturing or keeping these kinds of weapons, you call them criminals and you take military action against them.

(5) We also advise you to pack your luggage and get out of our lands. We desire for your goodness, guidance, and righteousness, so do not force us to send you back as cargo in coffins.

(6) Sixthly, we call upon you to end your support of the corrupt leaders in our countries. Do not interfere in our politics and method of education. Leave us alone, or else expect us in New York and Washington.

. . .

If you fail to respond to all these conditions, then prepare for fight with the Islamic Nation. The Nation of Monotheism, that puts complete trust on Allah and fears none other than Him. The Nation which is addressed by its Quran with the words:

. . .

So do not become weak (against your enemy), nor be sad, and you will be superior (in victory)if you are indeed (true) believers. [Quran 3:139]

The Nation of Martyrdom; the Nation that desires death more than you desire life:

Think not of those who are killed in the way of Allah as dead. Nay, they are alive with their Lord, and they are being provided for. They rejoice in what Allah has bestowed upon them from His bounty and rejoice for the sake of those who have not yet joined them, but are left behind (not yet martyred) that on them no fear shall come, nor shall they grieve. They rejoice in a grace and a bounty from Allah, and that Allah will not waste the reward of the believers. [Quran 3:169-171]

. . .

The Islamic Nation that was able to dismiss and destroy the previous evil Empires like yourself; the Nation that rejects your attacks, wishes to remove your evils, and is prepared to fight you. You are well aware that the Islamic Nation, from the very core of its soul, despises your haughtiness and arrogance.

If the Americans refuse to listen to our advice and the goodness, guidance and righteousness that we call them to, then be aware that you will lose this Crusade Bush began, just like the other previous Crusades in which you were humiliated by the hands of the Mujahideen, fleeing to your home in great silence and disgrace. If the Americans do not respond, then their fate will be that of the Soviets who fled from Afghanistan to deal with their military defeat, political breakup, ideological downfall, and economic bankruptcy.

This is our message to the Americans, as an answer to theirs. Do they now know why we fight them and over which form of ignorance, by the permission of Allah, we shall be victorious?

BIBLIOGRAPHY

Aboul-Enein, Youssef, LCDR, MSC, USN. "The Late Sheikh Abdullah Azzam's Books," The Combatting Terrorism Center, http://ctc.usma.edu/publications/publications.asp (accessed 24 November 2009).

Al Jazeera-Gallup Pakistan Survey, "Pakistan: State of the Nation," August 13, 2009, Aljazeera.net, http://english.aljazeera.net/ focus/2009/08/2009888238994769.html#threat (accessed August 12, 2009).

Alexiev, Alex. "Afghanistan at the Crossroads," *National Review Online* (February 23, 2010), Hudson Institute, http://www.hudson.org/index.cfm?fuseaction=publication_details&id =6784&pubType=HI_Opeds (accessed March 18, 2010).

Algar, Hamid. *Wahhabism: A Critical Essay.* Oneonta, NY: Islamic Publications International, 2002.

Ali, Maulana M. *The Holy Qur'an.* Dublin, Ohio: Ahmadiyya Anjuman Isha'at Islam Lahore Inc. U.S.A., 2002.

Altman, Israel Elad. "The Crisis of the Arab Brotherhood." *Current Trends in Islamist Ideology*, Volume 6 (November 29, 2007). Hudson Institute: Center on Islam, Democracy, and the Future of the Muslim World. http://www.currenttrends.org/research/detail/the-crisis-of-the-arab-brotherhood (accessed August 6, 2009).

Altman, Israel Elad. "Strategies of the Muslim Brotherhood Movement 1928-2007." *Research Monographs on the Muslim World*, Series No 2, Paper No 2. Hudson Institute: Center on Islam, Democracy, and the Future of the Muslim World, 2009.

Armstrong, Karen. *Islam: A Short History.* New York: Random House, 2002.

Bar, Shmuel. "Sources of Islamist Strategic Thought." *Research Monographs on the Muslim World*, Series No 2, Paper No 1. Hudson Institute: Center on Islam, Democracy, and the Future of the Muslim World, 2008.

Bennett, Tony, Lawrence Grossberg, and Meaghan Morris, eds., *New Keywords: A Revised Vocabulary of Culture and Society.* Oxford: Blackwell Publishing Ltd, 2005.

Bergen, Peter, James Fallows, Bruce Hoffman, and Steven Simon. "*Al Qaeda* Then and Now." In *Al Qaeda Now: Understanding Today's Terrorists*, edited by Karen J. Greenberg, 3-26. New York: Cambridge University Press, 2005.

Bergesen, Albert, ed. *The Sayyid Qutb Reader: Selected Writings on Politics, Religion, and Society.* New York: Routledge, 2008.

Bukay, David. *From Muhammad to Bin Laden: Religious and Ideological Sources of the Homicide Bombers Phenomenon.* New Brunswick: Transaction Publishers, 2008.

Burke, Jason. *Al-Qaeda: The True Story of Radical Islam.* London: I.B. Tauris & Co Ltd, 2006.

Campbell, Alastair. An Investigation into Islamic Fundamentalism and an Assessment of its Relationship with the Concept of *Jihad*. Master's thesis, Command and General Staff College, 1992.

Cline, Austin. "Ibn Taymiyyah: Profile and Biography," About.com - Agnosticism/Atheism, http://atheism.about.com/library/FAQs/islam/blfaq_islam_taymiyyah.htm (accessed 6 December 2009).

Cline, Austin. "Islam and Muslims: Kharijites," About.com: Agnosticism/Atheism, http://atheism.about.com/library/ FAQs/islam/blfaq_islam_kharijites.htm (accessed December 6, 2009).

Desai, Meghnad. *Rethinking Islamism: The Ideology of the New Terror.* London: I.B.Tauris & Co. Ltd, 2007.

Esposito, John L. *The Islamic Threat: Myth or Reality?* New York: Oxford University Press, 1995.

Gabriel, Richard A. *Muhammad: Islam's First Great General.* Norman: University of Oklahoma Press, 2007.

Gant, Jim, Major, US Army Special Forces. *One Tribe at a Time: A Strategy for Success in Afghanistan*, 2nd ed. Los Angeles: Nine Sisters Imports Inc, 2009.

Gohari, M.J. *The Taliban: Ascent to Power.* London: Oxford University Press, 2001.

Greenberg, Karen J., ed. *Al Qaeda Now: Understanding Today's Terrorists.* New York: Cambridge University Press, 2005.

Gunaratna, Rohan and Anders Nielsen. *"Al Qaeda* in the Tribal Areas Between Afghanistan and Pakistan." *Studies in Conflict & Terrorism* 31 (2008):775–807.

Gunaratna, Rohan. *Inside Al Qaeda: Global Network of Terror.* New York: Berkley Books, 2003.

Gvosdev, Nikolas K. and Ray Takeyh. *The Receding Shadow of the Prophet: The Rise and Fall of Radical Political Islam.* Westport: Praeger, 2004.

Habeck, Mary. *Knowing the Enemy: Jihadist Ideology and the War on Terror.* New Haven: Yale University Press, 2006.

Henzel, Christopher. "The Origins of al Qaeda's Ideology: Implications for US Strategy," *Parameters*, Spring 2005, 69-80.

Hoffman, Bruce. *Al Qaeda*, Trends in Terrorism and Future Potentialities: An Assessment. RAND paper, The RAND Corporation, Washington, D.C., 2003.

Huband, Mark. *Warriors of the Prophet: The Struggle for Islam.* Boulder: Westview Press, 1999.

Inskeep, Steve. "Shifting Language: Trading Terrorism for Extremism." NPR.com, July 27, 2005. http://www.npr.org/templates/story/story.php?storyId=4772826 (accessed April 13, 2010).

Jacquard, Roland. Samia Serageldin, ed. Translated by George Holoch. *In the Name of Osama Bin Laden: Global Terrorism and the Bin Laden Brotherhood.* London: Duke University Press, 2002.

Kepel, Gilles and Jean-Pierre Milelli, ed. Translated by Pascale Ghazaleh. *Al Qaeda in its Own Words.* Cambridge: Belknap Press of Harvard University Press, 2008.

Kepel, Gilles. Translated by Pascale Ghazaleh. *The War for Muslim Minds: Islam and the West.* Cambridge: Belknap Press of Harvard University Press, 2004.

Khadduri, Majid. *War and Peace in the Law of Islam.* Baltimore: The Johns Hopkins Press, 1955.

Lambton, Ann K.S. *State and Community in Medieval Islam.* Oxford: Oxford University Press, 1981.

Lawrence, Bruce, ed. Translated by James Howarth. *Messages to the World: The Statements of Osama Bin Laden.* London: Verso, 2005.

Lee, Robert D. *Overcoming Tradition and Modernity: The Search for Islamic Authenticity.* Boulder: Westview Press, 1997.

Lewis, Bernard. *The Crisis of Islam: Holy War and Unholy Terror.* New York: Modern Library, 2003.

Marquand, Robert. "The Tenets of Terror," *Christian Science Monitor* , csmonitor.com (October 18, 2001), http://www.csmonitor.com/2001/1018/p1s2-wogi.html (accessed December 6, 2009).

Mitchell, Richard S. *The Society of the Muslim Brothers.* New York: Oxford University Press, 1993.

Moreau, Ron and Sami Yousafzai. "Turning the Taliban." *Newsweek*.com (February 12, 2010). http://www.newsweek.com/id/233590?obref=obnetwork (accessed March 25, 2010).

Muthuswamy, Moorthy S. *Defeating Political Islam: The New Cold War.* Amherst, NY: Prometheus Books, 2009.

Musallam, Adnan A. *From Secularism to Jihad: Sayyid Qutb and the Foundations of Radical Islamism.* Westport: Praeger, 2005.

"Muslim Brotherhood: The Roots of the Pan-Islamic *Jihad*," Tell Children the Truth, http://www. tellthechildrenthetruth.com/mbhood_en.html (accessed 6 December 2009).

O'Neill, Bard E. *Insurgency & Terrorism: From Revolution to Apocalypse.* 2nd ed. Washington, DC: Potomac Books, Inc., 2005.

Obama, Barack. Presidential Address to the Nation on the Way Forward in Afghanistan and Pakistan, United States Military Academy at West Point, West Point, NY, December 01, 2009.

Palmer, Monte and Princess Palmer. *Islamic Extremism: Causes, Diversity, and Challenges.* Lanham, MD: Rowman & Littlefield Publishers, 2008.

Pavlin, James. "Ibn Taymiyya, Taqi al-Din (1263-1328)," Islamic Philosophy Online, http://www. muslimphilosophy. com/ip/rep/H039.htm (accessed 6 December 2009).

Perry, Mark. *Talking to Terrorists: Why America Must Engage with its Enemies.* New York: Basic Books, 2010.

Peters, Ralph. Guest lecture, Command and General Staff College, Fort Leavenworth, KS, March 10, 2010.

Qutb, Sayyid. Translated by John. B. Hardie. *Social Justice In Islam.* Revised edition. Oneonta, NY: Islamic Publications International, 2000.

Rashid, Ahmed. *Taliban: Militant Islam, Oil and Fundamentalism in Central Asia.* New Haven: Yale University Press, 2001.

Riedel, Bruce. *The Search for Al Qaeda: Its Leadership, Ideology, and Future.* Washington, DC: Brookings Institution Press, 2008.

Sageman, Marc. *Understanding Terror Networks.* Philadelphia: University of Pennsylvania Press, 2004.

Scheuer, Michael. "Al-Qaeda's Military Chief in Afghanistan Views the Ongoing Insurgency with Optimism." *Terrorism Focus*, Volume 5, Issue 28 (July 29, 2008). http://www.jamestown.org (accessed December 10, 2009).

Scheuer, Michael. "Al-Qaeda's New Leader in Afghanistan: A Profile of Abu al-Yazid." *Terrorism Focus*, Volume 4, Issue 21, July 3, 2007. http://www.jamestown.org (accessed 21 August 2009).

Scheuer, Michael. *Through Our Enemies' Eyes: Osama Bin Laden, Radical Islam, and the Future of America*. Washington, DC: Brassey's Inc., 2003.

Tanner, Stephen. *Afghanistan: A Military History from Alexander the Great to the War Against the Taliban*. Updated version. Philadelphia: Da Capo Press, 2009.

The Jamestown Foundation. "Al-Qaeda in Afghanistan Urges Professionals to Joint Mujahideen," Terrorism Focus, Volume 5, Issue 11 (March 18, 2008). http://www.jamestown.org (accessed December 10, 2009).

Wiktorowicz, Quintan. "Anatomy of the *Salafi* Movement," *Studies in Conflict & Terrorism* 29 (2006): 207-239.

Wiktorowicz, Quintan. "A Genealogy of Radical Islam ." *Studies in Conflict & Terrorism* 28 (2005): 75-97.